REFLECT

THE CHELMER & BLACKWATER NAVIGATION

NAVIGATION

TWELVE MONTHS – TWELVE MOODS

HISTORY & IMAGINATION

ILLUSTRATED

THE LITTORAL PRESS

By the same author:

Photographs: Clare Harvey

REFLECTIONS

To Gareth
Best Wishes
Mervyn

June 2005.

MERVYN LINFORD

THE LITTORAL PRESS

First Published in 2005

The Littoral Press
38 Barringtons, 10 Sutton Rd,
Southend-on-Sea, Essex SS2 5NA
United Kingdom

British Library Cataloguing-in-Publication Data
A catalogue record of this book is available
From the British Library

ISBN 09541844-4-0

Printed by 4Edge Ltd. Hockley, Essex.

CONTENTS

THE CHELMER & BLACKWATER NAVIGATION

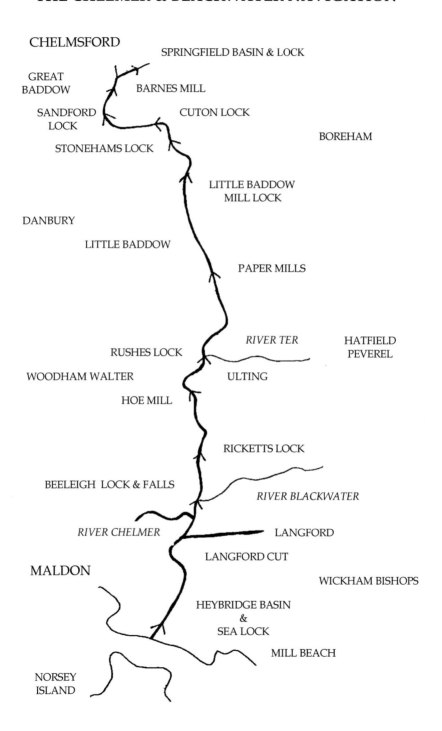

CHELMSFORD

SPRINGFIELD BASIN & LOCK

GREAT
BADDOW
BARNES MILL

SANDFORD
LOCK
CUTON LOCK

STONEHAMS LOCK
BOREHAM

LITTLE BADDOW
MILL LOCK

DANBURY

LITTLE BADDOW

PAPER MILLS

RIVER TER
HATFIELD
PEVEREL

RUSHES LOCK

WOODHAM WALTER
ULTING

HOE MILL

RICKETTS LOCK

BEELEIGH LOCK & FALLS

RIVER BLACKWATER

RIVER CHELMER
LANGFORD

LANGFORD CUT

MALDON
WICKHAM BISHOPS

HEYBRIDGE BASIN
&
SEA LOCK

MILL BEACH

NORSEY
ISLAND

INTRODUCTION

CHELMER NAVIGATION

Amble along the Chelmer's paths –
The old ways, haunted by harness
And the toll of hooves.

Stroll where the barges
Used to brush the banks –
Where the brambles
Tumble to the water's edge.

Wade through the mallow
In its swathes of mauve,
To where the long grown grass
Sprawls over iron
Onto crumbled brick;

And the air, pervasive
With the weight of years,
Carries its cargo
Through the lock's slow timbre.

The Beginning of the 'Long Pond' Beeleigh

After many years and many failed proposals and attempts the Chelmer and Blackwater Navigation was finally completed on June 3rd 1797. The canal is still owned, maintained and run, by The Company of The Proprietors of the Chelmer and Blackwater Navigation Limited, who have the distinction of being the only company in control of a fully navigable canal in England that they actually built themselves in the first place. The greatest hindrance to the building of the navigation was the opposition to its construction by the townspeople of Maldon who rightly feared a loss of trade and employment in their own maritime industry. Eventually after many decades of opposition a scheme was drawn up by the ninth Lord Petre of Ingatestone and Thomas Branston MP of Skreens, Roxwell which overcame the 'Maldon Problem' by proposing a new channel that would bypass the town altogether . A sea lock was proposed at what was to become Heybridge Basin, large enough to accommodate shipping which would moor off Collier's Reach in the Blackwater Estuary. At the other end of the canal a second basin was proposed for Springfield rather than in the Chelmsford parish and a short cut was to connect the basin with the river below Moulsham Mill. Although opposition to the navigation never abated Royal assent to the Chelmer navigation Bill was finally given on the 17th of June 1793. The first meeting of the owners of the proposed canal was held in the Black Boy Hotel in Chelmsford on July the 15th 1793 and construction started later that year under the overall direction of the famous engineer, John Rennie, who was also responsible for the building of the Kennet and Avon Canal where the design of the locks and bridges are remarkably similar to those on the Chelmer and Blackwater Navigation itself. He is said to have only visited the site five times and the actual river survey was completed by one Charles Wedge. Day to day control of the construction was given over to Richard Coates, a Yorkshire man, who had already worked under Rennie on the Ipswich to Stowmarket Navigation. The first brig sailed into Heybridge Basin on St Georges Day 1796 and its arrival was reported in the Chelmsford Chronicle with the words ' ... *there arrived in the grand basin at the entrance of the Chelmer Navigation, near Collier's Reach, the good brig Fortunes Increase, Robert Parker, master, laden with 150 chaldrons of the best Burnmore coals from Sunderland consigned to messrs Blyth and Coates, the first adventurers on the navigation'.* The brig was the first of many to use the navigation and over the next six months the canal was slowly extended in stages until in September 1796 two barges loaded with foreign wheat reached Moulsham Mill just downstream of the town – the remainder of the canal was not fully completed until June the 3rd 1797. The total length of the canal is 13.75 miles with twelve locks that lift the water by some 77 feet between Maldon and Chelmsford. It carried many cargoes including: wheat, coal, coke, lime, chalk, slate and timber and continued to be prosperous until superseded by the building of the railway in the 1840's – which ironically, was constructed with materials brought in by barges on the canal itself! Richard Coates settled in Chelmsford after the completion of the canal and his businesses were eventually taken over by his nephew Brown who set up Brown and Sons, the once well known Timber and Builder's Merchants. Industry flourished in and around Chelmsford because of the canal and the first inland gas works in Britain was built in Chelmsford using coal barged up the navigation. Just downstream of Hoe Mill there once stood Britain's first sugar factory, a reminder of which can still be seen in the shape of the riverside cottages built for the workers. The first place to produce paper in Essex was Paper Mills at Little Baddow. There were two mills there, one for grinding corn and the other for pulping rags. Horse drawn barges used the canal until well into the 1950's and the last motorised vessels carrying timber from Heybridge Basin to Brown and Sons at their Springfield Depot finally ceased trading in 1972. Recent developments on the canal include: the restoration of Springfield Basin by the Inland Waterways Association in 1993, the repair of locks and bridges along the canal, facilitated by a Heritage

Lottery Grant in 1998 and the construction of a new marina north of Springfield Basin with moorings for 12 craft together with a new housing development overlooking the river. Future plans envisage a new marina at Sandford Mill utilising a disused water works with a new cut connecting it to the navigation; dredging and reopening the cut between Langford and Beeleigh falls to allow river access to the mill where a landing stage is planned; construction of a second marina at Springfield due to be started in 2005, and to extend the navigation into Chelmsford town centre by excavating another cut between Springfield Basin and the River Chelmer. The finance for this project is hoped to come from the redevelopment of the old gas works site in conjunction with Chelmsford Council and the proposed scheme could include a major hotel development and another marina. All in all it seems that The Chelmer and Blackwater Navigation Company is in good hands and that the prospects for an exciting future are more or less secure. I for one, having spent the last fifty years intimately involved with the navigation and the surrounding area, am grateful for that and look forward to spending what time I have left on earth reliving my past memories of the Chelmer and Blackwater Navigation, enjoying the rural charm of the present throughout the changing seasons, and looking forward to as much of a future beside the canal as God and reasonable health will allow.

CHELMSFORD

The county town of Chelmsford is a busy, typically modern 21st century town within easy commuting distance of London; although of great antiquity much of the town was destroyed in the Second World War – and it has to be said; by insensitive developers as well. In Roman times settlements grew up along the road connecting London to Colchester and Norwich including one at Moulsham known as Caesaromagus – the only Roman town in Britain to include the Emperor's title. It appears that the Romans left sometime in the 4th century after the collapse of the bridge across the river. The site of the present town was then uninhabited marshland between two rivers – the Can and the Chelmer. When the Saxons settled in the area they had little need of roads and their main trade passed through Writtle which became an important market town mainly because it had an easier crossing place over the River Can. Chelmsford's present history began c1100 when Bishop Maurice bridged the Can thus restoring the Roman road. In 1199 King John granted permission for a market on land between the Can and the Chelmer – now the site of the present High Street. This new centre of trade slowly merged with Moulsham village and as a consequence the importance of Writtle gradually declined until the market there eventually ceased altogether.

As far as geology is concerned Chelmsford lies roughly at the meeting point where the boulder clay from north Essex comes up against the London clay stretching up from the Thames estuary. At Danbury and elsewhere there are outcrops of Bagshot sands and due to the action of meltwater and river movements at the end of the last Ice Age the area is admirably supplied with sand and gravel deposits. Such a varied soil profile made it an important agricultural area with Chelmsford as its natural centre. Allied to that, the plentiful supply of flowing water facilitated the creation of many flourishing industries including: milling, brewing and tanneries. Being close to the 'Great Essex Road' Chelmsford naturally developed into a centre of administration and by the 18th century it had become an important stopping point for mail travelling from London to Sudbury, Bury St Edmunds, Harwich, Colchester and Norwich, amongst other places. It has been recorded that even in the 18th century the fastest mail coaches could do the journey from London to Norwich in 10 hours and that this necessitated a change of horses

11

at about every 12 miles! Chelmsford was well able to cater for this trade with its many coaching inns and stabling facilities. In 1797 the River Chelmer was canalised between Chelmsford and the port of Maldon – or more correctly, Heybridge Basin, which was in close proximity to Collier's Reach on the River Blackwater. In the 1840's the railway was built between London, Colchester and Norwich and the better communications augmented the already flourishing industries supported by the canal. Ironically the very canal that supplied much of the material to build the railway couldn't compete with this more modern system of communication and slowly died off as a consequence. In 1888 Chelmsford was granted a Royal Charter making it a municipal borough. Although Springfield and Widford stayed outside the borough boundaries, by the 1920's as the town expanded, they effectively became indistinguishable from their larger neighbour – along with places like: Great Baddow, Galleywood, Broomfield and Writtle. All these inconsistencies were eventually resolved by the 1974 boundary changes in England when Chelmsford Borough and the surrounding Rural District were amalgamated. And what of the future? Although Chelmsford is the county town and has both a university and a cathedral, it is still not classed as a city. Whether or not this oversight will ever be rectified is uncertain at the present moment in time, but one thing's for sure, situated as it is on the main communication routes between London and all the important towns and cities of East Anglia, its continued prosperity seems well and truly assured.

Collier's Reach

Springfield Basin

Thames barges at Maldon

Barnes Mill

Riverside Inn – Victoria Road Chelmsford

Cruisers - Sandford

15

Sandon

Danbury Ridge from north of the navigation

Great Baddow

A COLD CONFINEMENT

Not yet the pale
Drop-headed flower
To hatch regardless
From its shell of crystal.

The sun floats pallid
In unhurried albumen –
Settles on a slow fertility.

Trees are umbilical –
Veined and corded
To the earth's placenta,
And life bud-fisted
Like a coiled foetus.

Not yet through soil
Rocks the first contraction,
Where pain lies frozen
In a womb held dormant.

No birth conceived of
In this cold confinement:
Water is cryptic
Under still translucence –

Air, ice-heavy
Like an anaesthetic,
And light, low-rested
From its heaving rhythms.

A MURDER OF CROWS

In between the close of Christmas
And the promise of New Year
Time insisted on a cerement made of snow;
Where the month's declining hours
Turned the temperature severe
And the river lost its willingness to flow.

Plovers crossed the cloudless heavens
In a semaphore of flight
To evade the cold commitment of the east;
Where the wiles of the weather
Dazzled everything in sight
And transformed the southern lowlands into piste.

The solidity of water
Gripped the willow by its hair
And Delilah was the treason in the wind;
Every psalm in winter's Psalter
Antithetical to prayer
As the crows explained the reason why they sinned.

It was cold as death and darkening
To a firmament of stars
That would turn their iridescence into ice;
Where the frost began to sparkle
Like the powdering of glass
And the season wound the handle on the vice.

Such a night beyond defiance
As the moon assailed the skies
Like a snowball that the void somehow compressed;
Astronomical the science
That elucidated eyes
To the shiverings of venus in the west.

FROST APPLES

The apple tree has lost its leaves:
The yellow fruits are luminous –
Are lanterns to the old wassailing ghosts
Whose forms we see evolving from our breath.

The fieldfares and the redwings, less deceived,
Just scavenge through the windfalls in the frost:
A phantom moon hangs gibbous in the east –
Epiphany in blue before the stars

The New Year came with snow – lots of snow. The river by
Ulting church was frozen to a depth of about six inches and the
trailing branches of willows and alders were locked within its
iron grip. Fieldfares chacked as they plundered the berries on the
hawthorn and a robin sang its lonely, plangent song. There
would be no fishing today – but it didn't matter. It was enough to
walk beneath the snow-hung, vaulted cathedral of the trees. To
listen to the almost silence, the crystal voices of winter's pristine
angels. Janus was looking both ways – towards Boreas and the
Northern Lights and then forward to Flora and the blossoming of
spring. 'If winter comes, can spring be far behind'. Snow had
drifted to a depth of five feet in places. It lolled over the hedge
banks like the fluted gills of enormous toadstools or else the
flukes and fins of Arctic whales and dolphins. The wind lifted it
in loose veils and it blew across the river meadows like a white
and ghostly smoke. Smoke without heat – icicles hung from the
church eaves like diamante daggers and the thin whisper of the
icy wind whistled through wires and the frigid branches. In the
lee of a small copse and a hawthorn thicket snowdrops reared
their delicate heads in a nodding white defiance of the blizzard.
Snowdrop – flower of hope and purity - *Galanthus nivalis: gala*
'milk' and *anthos* 'flower': *Nivalis* meaning 'snow white' or

'growing near snow'. Hope is surely what they bring. A blackbird scratches in the dry leaves beneath a hedge and despite the white-out a stormcock rattles its early song from the top of a tall oak.

Twelfth Night is nearly upon us, the snow has thawed temporarily and the sun casts a low and unholy light across the river and the cattle meadows. Canada geese clamour in long skeins as they fly towards their refuge in the lakes beside Hoe Mill. Are they the loose unwritten lines of a long-forgotten language - a missive from Hades, as like all the hounds of the infernal regions they quicken the heartbeat with their clangourous voices? The surrounding farmland is a winter patchwork of brown and green. Some of the rich earth has been newly ploughed and the shining furrows stretch their glint and narrowing perspective into the blue and misted distance. Here and there acres of oil-seed rape and winter wheat add a warming verdancy, belying the stark anatomical coldness of the skeletal trees. Flocks of lapwing are flying high and towards the east – the green plover: Latin, *pluvia,* rain; old French, *plovier,* rainbirds – portentous of inclement weather. Twelfth Night – the eve of Epiphany. Once a time of great merriment, when the Bean King was appointed, the child who found the bean in the Twelfth Night cake: It seems that the celebrations derive from the festival of Saturnalia in old Roman times which was held at the same season. In the Julian calendar Twelfth Night is Old Christmas Day. It's just before midnight on January the 5th and I'm walking along the tow path at Hoe Mill. The constellation of Orion straddles the starry vault and a slight frost powders the rooftops and the shivering grasses. Christ will be manifest to the gentiles, Epiphany is at hand. Stars and the hook of a new moon still to a tremor in the river's velvet; one of the stars is brighter than the rest – Sirius perhaps, I'm not sure – and like Caspar, Melchoir and Balthazar, I feel the need to follow its shimmering trajectory. Anything is possible on a night like this; the occasional meteorite blazes into life and then disappears just as suddenly. The croak of a moorhen and the high pitched cry of a coot puncture the mysterious darkness and the temporal world of ice and misted water reasserts itself. Dream or reality – who's to know? Everything's an epiphany, the leafless trees, the moorhen and the coot, me even! All is the manifestation of the mind of God, we are God and God is us, all is one, all is an illusion; a fantastic, unbelievable, wonderful illusion. I can hear the water funnelling into the mill pool; can see it sparkle in the darkness as starlight and moonlight fracture its surface with their splintered silver. Midnight approaches and the Gregorian and Julian calendar meet in the moon-glade to relive Old Christmas. Old Father Christmas walks through the thickets of my imagination wreathed in ivy and mistletoe, a fox barks and the old wassailing ghosts lift their cups and drink my health with cider. Christmas is over, Yule is over, the winter solstice is behind us and Candlemas beckons with crocuses and coltsfoot. Clouds have started to cross the moon, the wind is picking up from the south west and the frost is melting. The 'rainbirds' were right, a depression is heading our way from the far Atlantic and a storm is brewing – rain will be here by morning.

There is rain and there is rain! For three days there has been an almost continuous drench from the scuds of cloud and the blustering sou'westers. The river has burst its banks and the extensive flood meadows have become an inland sea. Sporadic bushes stipple the surface of the swirling, viscous waters and seagulls dip and dive and screech in white battalions. Pike and perch roam across the unaccustomed bed of a widening river in search of worms and grubs and each other! The domestic geese that managed to survive Christmas are hunched up against the rain and wind beside their inundated grazing land. A pair of swans foreground a contrast as their strong down-reaching wings whistle and ring across the bleak and leaden skyways. The road is impassable at Hoe Mill and I walk across the raised wooden walkway as the thick and muddy water swirls violently beneath me. On one side of me the lock keeper's cottage is cut off and on the other a raging torrent spills across the fields and into the lakes by the gravel working. Where are the dove and the raven – the olive branches? Noah would recognise the scene; Danbury Ridge is Mount Ararat, St Mary the Virgin at Little Baddow, the Ark.

After three days and nights the rain finally stops. An Anticyclone is building over Scandinavia and the wind has turned into the east. It's Friday night and starlit and the temperature is plummeting. By midnight the frost is as thick as snow on the grass and the river is freezing over. Dawn, Saturday, and the air is as cold and dense as the ice itself. The sun contracts from red to liquid gold and all is blue and white and gilded mist. I drive down to the bridge below Boreham and park the car. Acres of flooded meadows have turned to ice overnight and already one or two hardy individuals have donned their skates and are glissading across the scintillating surfaces. I stand on the bridge and throw pebbles onto the frozen river. The hollow reverberations echo in the misted silence and a peewit cuts the air with cries and razor wings. Was that a peregrine falcon I saw stooping towards Danbury Ridge? They used to over-winter in the Chelmer and Blackwater valleys – perhaps they still do! By noon the temperature is still below freezing and there are dozens of parked cars and people skating everywhere. Even I give it a go – not with skates, just in my everyday shoes. It's exhilarating; I slide and turn, and crouch and jump and spin. I am connected to the weather. I am water, the mist is water vapour; the ice is solid water. I commune with hydrogen and oxygen – partake of the living element. Clouds block out the sun and it starts to snow – a thin, dry, easterly snow. People drift off home and I am left to the silence and the darkening landscape. There is a thin layer of powdery snow on the roads and the un-flooded fields. The moon between shower clouds is as golden as honey and the last diurnal light sinks into shadows and a robin's lamentations. Solstice, Christmas, Yule, Twelfth Night, Old Christmas and Epiphany: All have come and all have gone, the cycles repeat themselves, Life turns into death, light into dark, autumn into winter. 'If winter comes, can spring be far behind'? I drive towards home again. The thin snow is falling harder. I pass the church of St Mary the Virgin in Little Baddow; the snow drifts across my headlights with a spectral eeriness and the Christmas ghosts of untold centuries whisper their vespers by the amelanchier in the dark and frosted graveyard. I begin to think about the history of The Chelmer & Blackwater Navigation; of all the many mills and locks, and of all the people who spent their lives within earshot of harness bells, wildfowl, waterwheels and millstones.

Originally there were some 8 mills along the River Chelmer – If you count the long-gone ancient mill at Beeleigh Abbey – before the Navigation was constructed. Many of the millers were concerned that the alteration to the river's flow would affect their businesses adversely; this turned out not to be the case and in fact all the mills expanded considerably and their output increased accordingly. On April the 26th 1796 a barge was loaded with 150 sacks of flour at Hoe Mill bound for Heybridge Basin where it was off-loaded into a waiting vessel and transported to London. Over the next few years many tons of flour were shipped out of the ever-expanding mills as they took advantage of the easier communications afforded by the Navigation. Nowadays there are only a couple of mills surviving along the canal (Moulsham and Barnes Mill) and one by the River Blackwater at Langford; none of which are now used for their original purposes. Most of the other mills have long since disappeared, most of them having been burnt to the ground at one time or another. Paper Mills – as its name suggests – consisted of two mills, one carrying out the normal miller's trade and the other pulping rags for paper making. The site of Britain's first working sugar factory to the east of Hoe Mill is now overgrown and unrecognisable and the only real evidence of its former existence is a line of cottages known as 'Sugar Mill Cottages' alongside the Navigation between Hoe Mill and Ricketts lock. Most of the bridges, locks and lock houses, were built of local bricks made at Ulting, Boreham and Sawpit Field, and the capping material used was Dundee stone chosen for its weather-resistant durability. Horse-drawn barges were a common sight on the canal up until the mid 1950's and I consider myself fortunate to have seen them with my own eyes when I was a boy of about 8 or 9 years old. In the early days various types of sailing vessel could enter Heybridge Basin through the sea lock and unload their cargoes directly into the canal lighters, but as steam ships came into prominence in the early part of the 20th century many of them were too large to enter the lock and their cargoes were unloaded into de-masted Thames barges in the tidal Blackwater Estuary and then transferred to the basin for reloading onto working canal craft. In the 1960's the sea lock was lengthened to 130 feet and larger, timber-laden motor vessels could once again enter the basin and tranship their cargoes directly onto the canal lighters as used to be the case in the early days of the Navigation. Although the canal has long ceased to be a mercantile venture there are still many barges and motor cruisers using the canal for recreational purposes. Most of these are moored at Sandford lock, Paper Mills and Hoe Mill, and what with boating, angling, canoeing, rambling and the natural history and farming activities of the area it looks as though this little known, secluded corner of rural England will be attracting devotees of all persuasions for many years to come.

Ulting churchyard January

Ulting churchyard looking north

26

Sandford lock

Lock keeper's cottage – Hoe Mill

Bumfords Lane

Ulting

CONTRAST

The contrast of the blackbirds in the snow
Is something that composes in the mind
An icy thought. Of people long ago

Through fields of white – who trudged the bitter edge
Of all they knew and felt the bite of hunger –
Far from home. The hunters through the hedgerows

And the heath who prayed to gods unnumbered
In the cold – to warm their flesh. What pledges
Could the deities then keep – when under

Frost's dominion they patrolled the moment
That was ghosted on their breath? The thought's defined
At last. Blackbirds in the branches strike a pose –

Reminding us through windows in the sun
That winter: comes between us – like a wedge.

SNOWSEARCH

Like children we were –
Miles in secret to discover whiteness.
We stopped by a river in the drifted snowscape:
Made tracks, like music, through the muted meadows
And laughed at the lyric of our simple passion –
Saw grass, like footnotes, in the tufted margins
As hares loped hillward into blue-black spinneys.

Here, it was winter –
Not harsh like iron into ice destructive,
But soft and broken into white and water.
The sun in cirrus settled to westward, like a fire faded
And our hearts sank homewards into cold compliance.

SUNSTRUCK

Distances were drear. Lapwings roamed across
The misted fields and greenness disappeared
In banks of grey. Light was at a loss

And left unclear – where sky came down to earth
As damp as rain and moistened every minute
With its tears. There was a chill that curses

Could explain – as if the witch of winter
Cast a spell – denying at a breath the birth
Of spring. Unexpectedly a glint

Of slanted gold gave everything a gloss
Beneath the sun – and calmed our fears.
A warm angelic order free of frost

Exhumed the dying moment from its hearse
And turned our eyes to summer – at a squint.

Candlemas, and the Goddess returns from the Otherworld. Snowdrops 'the fair maids of spring' speak of the pagan festival of Imbolc – from the old name Oimelc; meaning ewe's milk – and the first lambs bleat in the distant meadows. Candelmas, The Purification of the Blessed Virgin Mary; that's now become The Presentation of Christ at the Temple, the time when the candles are blessed for the rest of the year. Down Bumfords Lane at Ulting the first coltsfoot are showing on the roadside verges, like sprites or nature's yellow imps lifting their floral crew-cuts for some early vernal mischief. Dandelions – *dent de lion;* tooth of lion – attract the first over-wintering tortoiseshells from the dusty corners of garden sheds and if you're lucky you may see a peacock butterfly flashing its eye markings from the golden florets in the welcome February sunlight. You may even see the brimstone, the insect that gave butterflies their name due to its rich buttery colour. In Ulting churchyard the first celandine show amongst the snowdrops and the resident blackbirds and thrushes welcome the miniature suns with bursts of sporadic song. A chaffinch finishes its lyric with a strident rattle, like a gush sparks emitting from its red-resplendent breast. Molehills stipple the sward and as if in sympathy crocuses shoulder the soil and bourgeon into light. Is it all too good to be true? 'February fill the dyke, be it black or be it white'! The river's still cold; the roach are lying deep and harder to catch than ever and last year's rushes are a tangle of brown and dishevelled decay. At night the frosts are still as sharp as ever and mornings find the margins splintered with fingers of ice. 'Be it black or be it white'; the wind is rising and in the east and a veil of high cirrus is moving up from the south. Low pressure over northern France and high pressure over northern Europe, it won't be black and that's for sure, the lapwings are travelling west and the tang of Siberia nips at the nose and the nostrils.

1963, the coldest winter last century they say, even colder than 1947 but perhaps not quite as snowy. But snow there was for the snow lover, and plenty of it. The Chelmer valley was like an Arctic wasteland. Snow drifted over hedges, lanes were blocked, and life and nature seemed at a virtual standstill. I was 17 years old and I remember coming to fish at Hoe Mill with my dear departed friend and mentor 'Slasher Martin'. He was the father of friends of mine and he taught me all I knew about angling and the natural environment – and I loved him dearly. We parked on the bridge by Hoe Mill lock and went to investigate the river. The ice was that thick that we could walk across the river at will, in fact I would vouch that it was that thick that we could have even driven the car across it if we'd felt so inclined! We attacked it with hammers and spikes and monkey wrenches, but to no avail – it was hopeless. And then we heard it – the tinkling trickle of running water. Where was it coming from – how could it be in this frozen wilderness? Water was seeping out under the ice from the lock gates and beneath the bridge there was about ten foot of unfrozen river. We tackled up and fished from the concrete aprons either side of the bridge. We couldn't go wrong; what with the available oxygen in the open water and the fishes need for food after such a prolonged freeze up – they were ravenous. Roach, dace, perch and chub, came to the net at frequent intervals and the fishing that day – even though it was perishing cold – was better than I've had on any occasion in June, July or August. Some may think it cruel to take advantage of the fish under such inclement circumstances, but the more I think about it the more I feel that we probably saved a lot of fish from near certain death by virtue of the amount of groundbait and loose feed we used in what was in all honesty their hour of greatest need.

Let's get back to more recent times. The snow has started to fall again. Soft bridal veils of whiteness drift across the sterile landscape as the virgin looks for a lover. The womb of the earth is warm but the skin is bitter. The wires that once held swallows sing their Siberian dirges and Ulting Lane begins to fill with snow. Danbury Ridge has disappeared and in the lull of the wind all is an immensity of silence. I'm in a crystal ball; I am both past and future and the present is timeless. Have you ever been alone in a whiteout – completely alone? Can you imagine Scott and Amundsen – the fear and the excitement, the hope and the despair? Imagine our antecedents traipsing the glacial moraine in search for food – praying to their ancient gods; ghosted by their own breath? A skein of Canada geese clank and clamour as they drag their ghostly chains and a shelduck – a refugee from the not too distant saltings – laughs its lost and eerie laugh. Icicles hang from the eaves of the sugar factory cottages and the black overarching water main whitens its reflection in the river. I love to walk the towpath in the virgin snow. I make my way to

33

Ricketts lock and the hump-backed two hundred year old brick bridge cradles my weight as I gaze into the back stream and the spinney. Here in early autumn I fished for roach with elderberries as the leaves created a red and gold mosaic on the river's surface. I went blackberrying with summer still well and truly in my mind. But now – what now? I can hear plainsong on the wind; Gregorian chants from a spectral Beeleigh Abbey. It is cold – so cold. The Roman legionnaires curse their luck in Maldon. Byrthnoth stands on the causeway to Norsey Island and eternity marks his name. It is cold – so cold. The snow is falling as thick as mist and I can just make out the lights in Langford waterworks. It is getting dark and the shivering Blackwater flows towards Beeleigh and its tidal confluence. The Long Pond stretches to Heybridge Basin and Collier's Reach beyond the sea lock. I must make my way home; the wind is behind me, the snow is deeper and drifting. I pass under the water main and the canal-side cottages and come to the wooden footbridge. I walk through a copse in the fathoming darkness and snow dislodges from the branches and showers me with manna. The car waits in a lay-by in Ulting Lane; it has been iced, like a Christmas cake, decorated by the Ice Queen. The Purification of the Virgin; Candelmas, Imbolc: it is time to seek shelter, to present myself at the hearth as Christ was presented at the temple – to warm the immortal soul by the fires of life and the heat of love eternal.

Not that the material world is any less important. To have a hearth at all you need a home and even a home is itself an expression of nature. There are many materials needed to build houses and the necessary infrastructure that goes with them and the Chelmer valley provides two of the most important ingredients – sand and gravel. During the Ice Age the Glacial ice sheets came as far south as a line drawn along the A12 from Romford through Chelmsford to a point somewhere near the west of Colchester. At the southern edge of the ice there was a lot of glacial meltwater pouring off and the sand and flint mixed up in the ice spread out to form vast beds of gravel. Action from rivers and streams resorted some of the beds and formed a number of sand and gravel river terraces. So there you have it; when you look at the mortar in your brickwork, the glass in your windows, the concrete in your foundations and the surrounding roads, you can rest assured that the Ice Age was at least partly responsible for your wellbeing! There are a number of ex sand and gravel workings along the navigation and those I am most familiar with are the ones beside the river at Hoe Mill. When I was a teenager the sound of gravel being graded was a constant accompaniment to fishing, bird-watching and nature study in general. Nowadays the machinery has gone silent and what we are left with are a couple of large lakes either side of the road that have matured beautifully and now blend in perfectly with the surrounding rural environment; and as an added bonus, they are also well stocked with fish!

'If winter comes, can spring be far behind'? The snow thawed about a week or so ago. Patches of whiteness lingered for a while by the hedgerows where it had drifted and on the north facing slopes of Danbury Ridge. The buds on the elder are almost ready to burst and an occasional swathe of red-dead-nettles and ground ivy show from the relative warmth of a few favoured places. Some of the resident birds seem more determined and confident about their singing. 'The wise thrush sings its song twice over' and the blackbird composes with a golden nib. Starlings are losing their bib of blizzards and are taking on their vernal iridescence. An ecstatic wren sings a song that belies its diminutive size and a dunnock's thin treble pierces the hedgerow with all the force of a Bunsen burner. Mallards take to the river and drakes in the throes of sexual passion near drown their prospective mates in a silvery thrash of instinctive water. Frogs croak frenetically in the nearby ponds and cling by the dozens to the hapless females. Newts come up for air, stare inanely; then submerge, sinuously, back from whence they came. Male sticklebacks gain red throats and sapphire eyes and get ready to be 'mothers' to their offspring. The dykes may yet fill with black or white, frost may be severe and even in March and April snow is not unheard of, but for now forsythia bursts from the garden fences like the gift of fire, crocuses open their golden gapes as the sun feeds them its scraps of early warmth and the daffodils split their protective seams ready to sample the sunlight and the bees. A pair of swans fly out across the meadows towards Rushes lock and the empurpled rooks are roisterous and revelling above the treetops. March is on its way; the first real month of spring, the harbinger of summer's longed for bounty. Soon, the days will be longer than the nights, the coarse season will close, the fish begin to spawn, ornithologists and 'twitchers' will reach for their binoculars and the ramblers take to the towpaths and the byways. Soon, the world will come alive – fully alive.

Weir pool – Paper Mills

Reflections - Ulting

Paper Mills lock & 'Bothy'

Snow on Hoe Mill bridge

The Mill House – Little Baddow

The Mill House garden

MARCH
POEMS:

OCCURRENCE

Always a shock, for days you look; nothing –
Nothing, save greens and greys
And the branch-bare season
Swaddled in ivy from its root of iron.

Truth is, you forget, a thrush sings
And you half remember,
But as yet there is silence
And a sense of winter.

And then, it happens:
The earth softens
And a crocus shudders into light –
Gold has been reinvented.

You start to notice:
A bee ignites the fuse of recognition;
Starlings turn their doubts to iridescence –
From every fence, forsythia explodes.

THE CHURCH OF LEAVES

The rooks remember spring – high in the trees
They carry sticks – bicker and banter.
The sunlight is serious and they believe

Entirely in their God. This is a sermon
From the sun – words of light – homilies
Of warmth. What can they do? Be as the birds

Have always been – prompt for the church of leaves –
Passionate in prayer. There's nothing absurd
In their religion – kingdom and keys

Are one – instinct – the liturgy. No cant
Disturbs their worship: theirs is a pure belief.
They do not need the righteousness of ranters –

For them there is the doctrine of the earth
And only worms – can bring them to their knees.

MARCH MORNING

This morning was another place –
Each blade of grass was bristling with frost
And every tree a ghost in rags of blue.

The fishpond was a white, obscuring glass
Allowing neither light nor any view
To pass beyond the censor of itself.

A chaffinch flew from branch to dipping branch
As if a spark were kindled out of ice
To chance the air made steamy by the sun;

And everywhere, the rumour that was spring
Was echoed by the blackbird and the thrush;
Until, by noon, the world had had enough
Of winter and its glittering attire.

St David's Day and the first daffodils are showing in some of the riverside gardens – especially those facing south. It's at times like these that I think of those archetypical English poets Herrick and Wordsworth. Both of them loved daffodils and wrote near perfect poems about them to prove their point. The word daffodil, also known colloquially as 'the Lent lily' is a corruption of the Greek word for the asphodel, a plant that grew in 'the meadows of Persephone'. As Persephone was the Queen of Hades it has always been associated with the dead and people used to lay bunches of the flowers on the graves of their dear departed loved ones. One wonders if the reason that the daffodil is thought unlucky in some regions is purely because of the way it hangs its head, or does it have something to do with its connection to the asphodel? Personally, I've never thought of it as being an unlucky plant and have always seen it as one of the most beauteous harbingers of warmer weather. I also think of Edward Thomas at about this time, of Welsh parentage and yet arguably one of the greatest poets of the English countryside that England has ever produced. Poetry and the English countryside is without doubt my *raison d'etre*. That I write poetry at all has much to do with the Chelmer, fishing, and what Jack Hargreaves called 'the angler's other eye'! St David's Day, a blue-unbounded sky, birdsong and the first apple and pear blossom in the orchards – who could not be a poet on a day like today? We're all poets at heart, if we could only give ourselves enough time to feel instead of being constantly engaged in thinking. The senses, the emotions, the feelings, we are as much these things as we are our thoughts. Allow nature to speak to you; just look and listen, it will – I promise. The blue-unbounded sky speaks of infinity. Birdsong harmonises with the 'music of the spheres' and the blossom in the orchards whispers of beauty and eternal love. There are of course two patron saint's days in the month – St David's and St Patrick's. I never forget St Patrick's Day on the 17th because both my mother's birthday and the start of the close season for fishing are on the 16th. This is the time when the resident birds really start singing in earnest. The great-tits double note rings through the woodlands like a change of bells. Charms of goldfinches tinkle in the hedgerows and moorhens and coots on the river rend the vernal silence with their harsh calls and strident bickering. The ubiquitous sparrows puff up their brown bravado and squabble round the eaves of Ulting Church and in the nearby trees starlings on the lookout for nesting holes – if they have not already found one – murmur continuously as they mimic their country brethren. There are finches everywhere: bullfinches blaze from the yet to blossom sloe bushes, chaffinches trill and rattle from the copses and linnets accompany them with their virtuoso performances. Who could not be a poet on days like these? The river sparkles in the sunlight all the way from the sea lock at Heybridge to Springfield Basin. At Beeleigh the Chelmer and the Blackwater meet and cascade like liquid silver over the weir into the tidal waters above Maldon. At Hoe Mill the mill pool catches the sun and shimmers like a gold doubloon. At Little Baddow bridge someone stands looking into their own reflection as an early canoe cuts through the scintillating surfaces like the sleek form of a mink or an otter. A water vole traverses the canal below Boreham and at Barnes Mill the ghost of a water wheel churns through the coruscating flow and drips its dazzling, spectral droplets into the aureate waters. Who could not be a poet on days like these? The blue-unbounded sky, the birdsong and the blossom in the orchards; time turns and yet is timeless, a shoal of roach cross my reflected image and my double self delves and deciphers in the fathomless realms of spirit.

March the 21st, the spring equinox – equal light and dark. The birch, hawthorn and elder are coming into leaf, grass begins to grow again and the corn is greening in the fields. This is the season of the alder, sacred to the God Bran whose head was buried beneath the White Tower in London to protect the nation from its enemies. The alder, so plentiful along the Chelmer/Blackwater Navigation, so evocative of fifty years of my river-happy, extraordinary life; being water resistant, piles made of alder were used for the foundation of bridges and Winchester Cathedral rests upon them to this very day! Robert Graves said that it was a sacred tree because when it was cut the white wood turned red as though it was bleeding. Now is the time that the first migrant birds appear; the chiff-chaff being the earliest, singing its eponymous and somewhat repetitious song from the willow plantations beside the river. Soon the willow warbler will join it, filling the warming air with its sweet and falling cadences. But don't be fooled, 'March many weathers' will surely live up to its name and nip the buds with frost, bend the willows with a westerly blast, or fill the burgeoning ditches with snow! After the ravages of Dutch elm disease a couple of decades ago there don't seem to be as many rookeries as there used to be beside the navigation; although there are still some here and there farther inland making use of alternative nesting sites. A 'parliament of rooks', is there anything more representative of March than these dark disciples of debate as they purple the airways with their boisterous iridescence? Lambs are bleating in the meadows, elderberries unfurl their spring-welcoming leaves and the first fish rise for the first hatch of flies – it is paradise regained, surely. In the fields of winter wheat mad March hares race around frenetically only stopping for bouts of impromptu boxing. A kestrel hovers, a sparrow hawk soars and a skylark climbs the ladder of its song. But the wind is turning north and Boreas is not yet beaten.

Nearly the end of the month and after a night of severe frost the shower clouds are starting to build over Hatfield Peverel to the north. The first outriders of yet another blizzard come in the form of large six-sided flakes drifting and swirling in a fitful breeze. The sky begins to darken over Nounsley and distances are suddenly obliterated. To the south Danbury Ridge is still visible but slowly begins to fade as the snow picks up momentum. The rooks have stopped squabbling, the skylark's song is silenced and Hopkin's famous 'windhover' has gone to roost. Who could be a poet on a day like this? I could, for one – I just love snow! The season is ruled by Venus but love will be cold today; passion must be curtailed until the onset of warmer weather. The hares have disappeared in a veil of enveloping whiteness and the snow's evolving blanket quietens the pheasant and the whirring partridge. I drive down to Hoe Mill bridge, park the car, get out, and then stand and listen. Nothing, complete and utter silence, except for the thin trickle of water as it seeps through the shivering lock gates. The moored up pleasure craft seem somehow incongruous in such an Arctic scene as this. I remember Mrs Kemp, lock keeper, fishing bailiff and general all round fount of piscatorial wisdom. How many winters did that wonderful woman spend by the cottage fire on her own as the snow blew round the eaves and drifted deeper up against her door? Is there a comparable river elsewhere – in the 'summerlands' perhaps? Does she issue day tickets to angels – tell them the best places to fish and the right species to go for? Probably, probably! Rest in peace Mrs Kemp – rest in peace. I can hear a muffled bell ringing from the church at Woodham Walter. The snow is getting lighter and a few breaks begin to appear in the clouds. Visibility returns and the sun begins to shine again. The sun is comparatively warm at the end of March and the lying snow begins to thaw immediately. It's pouring off the branches, glint, prismatic drops drenching and drowning as they near in-urn me. Hardy of course comes to mind: 'Snow in the Suburbs' – what a wonderful poem! It's time to go home again and I drive the long way round down Bumfords Lane and over the tops to Paper Mills and Little Baddow. The River Ter cuts through white fields as it makes its meandering way towards Rushes lock and weir pool. The rooks are flying again; black against thawing white and the sun-shot golden trees. Who could not be a poet on a day like this? We don't express the weather – the weather expresses us. We are the weather: the sun in the trees through photosynthesis nourishes our bodies, puts light in our bones; is the word incarnate, the love of the stars manifested in flesh. At Paper Mills the water that's tumbling over the weir is whiter than the rapidly disappearing snow. A skylark climbs ecstatically into the blue and heaven's golden gates are open wide. A chiff-chaff sings its repetitious song and an early willow warbler drops a falling cadence. Home – where is home? I could stay at Paper Mills forever – and who knows perhaps I will! Did the monks at Beeleigh Abbey know this feeling – this sense of oneness; of absolute belonging? Perhaps; perhaps not, but surely they knew the spring as well as I and thanked their God with eulogies of praise for love and the light and the glorious Lenten weather.

Much of Beeleigh Abbey was destroyed during and after the Dissolution and very little of it remains to be seen in the fields to the west of Maldon. The few monastic buildings that do still exist have been lovingly restored by the present owners and although not open to the public can still be seen from the lane that runs down to Beeleigh Falls. The abbey was founded in 1180 by Robert Mantell and was occupied by monks of the Premonstratensian Order – known more colloquially as the White Canons. The Order was established by St Norbert and named after a place near Laon in N.E. France where St Norbet built his first abbey. Two parts of the buildings that still remain intact are the dormitory and the refectory. The beautifully arched and spanned roof of the dormitory can still be seen but the building now houses books instead of monks! The sumptuous refectory is supported by slender columns of Purbeck marble and contains a splendid marble fireplace. The adjoining chapel – used as a pigsty until the 19th century – has now been reclaimed and contains a small organ said the have belonged to Handel; on which his famous 'Largo' was said to have been composed. The abbey's patrons and guardians were the Bourchier family – one time Earls of Essex. The family had donated many of the vestments used by the White Canons and they may well have attracted a certain 'interest' in the Commissioners at the Dissolution as they were decorated with the badges of the House of York. Both Henry Vll and Henry Vlll had tried to destroy the surviving branches of the House of York and yet here in 1536 was an Abbey still displaying Yorkist affiliations! Beeleigh Abbey has its own saint – St Roger Niger of 'Bileye'. He was probably one of the earliest members of the community when it was first settled in about 1185 and after his death and canonisation his heart was enshrined at the abbey's high altar. In 1507 a Maldon man – John Ormsby – added 'a relic of the Holy Cross of the Sepulchre of Christ and of the Crib and Stall of Christ, enclosed in beryl' to the collection of relics at Beeleigh and many people are believed to have made pilgrimages to worship the sacred artefacts. In 1540 – at the Dissolution – the abbey and its lands were granted to Sir John Gates, Chancellor of the Duchy of

'Lancaster' by Henry Vlll and it's said that Sir John still haunts the remaining buildings. The inventory at the Dissolution shows: byres, stables, a pigsty, sheep pens, and a mill, and 34 fields and 4 tracts of woodland were also granted to Sir John Gates – 'the Lancastrian'! Nowadays the remains of Beeliegh Abbey are approached by a narrow country lane but in earlier times it seems that there was some sort of boathouse on the south bank of the River Chelmer close to the abbey and that the White Canons and their visitors arrived and departed in rowing boats. Many's the time I've leant on the railings at the bottom of that particular country lane and looked out across the wide beds of phragmites reeds towards Fullbridge and the ancient, hilltop town of Maldon itself – and what a wonderful watery world it is. At high tide the River Chelmer floods across the mudflats and fills the hollows by the few houses along its banks. The water even flows through a channel under the lane and nearly makes a 'moated manor house' of a small wooden bungalow nestling in amongst the trees and the surrounding marshland. Further down the lane – by using a public right of way – you can walk right up to Beeleigh lock, weir and falls. Not, I hasten to add, a waterfall of any great magnitude, but nevertheless distinguished as being the only true waterfall in Essex. The tidal waters in the vicinity receive a considerable amount of freshwater at times and as a consequence I have caught some of by best roach, dace and chub in those boiling, brackish deeps! It's also there that the River Blackwater joins the River Chelmer and where 'The Long Pond' bypasses Maldon on its toll-pathed and willowy way towards Heybridge Basin and the Blackwater estuary beyond. One needs to be particularly lacking in soul or a sense of history and not still be able to feel the presence of the White Canons going about their timeless, daily business, especially when the river mist creeps across the marshes at dusk and the first resplendent stars speak of creation and the Word of God. You can still hear the long oars dipping into the eddying tidal waters and imagine the monks dressed all in white floating through the gathering darkness towards the vespers of the owls, and then on to compline, an all too brief rest before matins and another day of brotherly love and hard agricultural labour.

Bridge below Boreham

Beeleigh Abbey

River Ter – ford below Nounsley

Walkway above the weir - Beeleigh

Boreham

Hatfield Peverel

APRIL
POEMS:

LAPWINGS

Sometimes, when spring, like a green idea,
Dispenses with winter and its icy reason –
When the season's instinct
Proffers a flower to enamoured bees
And the leaves between showers
Whisper their secrets to flirtatious light;

Then may you see them, on the skittish air,
Those careless plovers
Cresting their passion on erratic wings –
High in their raptures of rhapsodic flight
As they climb, but to tumble
From the sun's seduction;

Then may you see them, in the wind's embrace
As they cry, like derision,
Over jilted pasture –
Where the sky, made frantic
By their fleet attention,
Clings, like a lover, to each thin proposal.

EASTER SUNDAY

The weeping cherry eases into bloom:
Over the daffodils – pink on the edge
Of gold. Long-forgotten is the gloom

Of former days – now that the sun increases
At a height and sheds its rays to wake
The blackbird's song. Suddenly there's peace –

The equinoctial gales no longer shake
The branches of the stark – denuded trees.
Everything is other than a fake –

The true denomination leaves the tomb
And spends its share of blessings – like a pledge.
The daffodils become the cherry's groom –

Where all the world's responses praise the east
And birds – cry out hosannas: from the hedge.

SWALLOW

The swallow complies with physics –
Is both wave and particle.

It follows on from air –
Visits awareness, like an apparition.

Fire and blue steel both –
Tempered by sunlight
And the slake of water.

Spirit and substance:
It flies to its dual ends –
Mind over matter to the tips of feathers.

A ghost in oscillations over wheat,
That resonates with everything that's summer.

April the 1st and the leaves are far from foolish. Most of the trees are coming into leaf; even the oak and ash are bursting at the bud. Elder, birch, weeping willow, plum, alder, sycamore, elm, hornbeam, apple, chestnut, willow, aspen, lime, horse chestnut, maple, poplar and beech – all speaking the immortal words of Browning: 'Oh to be in England now that April's here'. As the month progress the cuckoo flowers (lady's smock) and the first cuckoo will meet beside the sun-shafted river with double notes and pale-prophetic blooms. For now it is enough to listen to the arrival of migrants from the warm south. Willow warblers serenade the navigation from Sandford lock to Beeleigh and beyond. Rushes are coming into their own and sedge and reed warblers wind their ratchets beside the fish-fathoming river. Whitethroats sing their spring-sweet songs from the tops of bourgeoning bushes and the first swallows twitter as they skim the gilded waters of the river and the glint surrounding shimmer of the lakes. 'March winds and April Showers', what a glorious combination! The cumuli climb on the thermals into blue-begotten skies; the tops are glacial and golden edged and the bottoms are black and pregnant with precipitation. April rain – is there anything more delightful? Sun-scattered crystal droplets, splitting the secrets of light with their prismatic edgeless edges! Smell the newly moistened earth and the wet vegetation – is it not sweeter than the most expensive perfume? Look to the skies as the spectrum arcs from horizon to horizon and the swallow's trajectory follows the rainbow to the season's crock of treasure. Fish are rising; insects are hatching, and daffodils and narcissi colour the copses and the cottage gardens. Various trees, both known and unknown - even to me - are blossoming in profusion: pinks and whites of both wild and ornamental species beautify the hedgerows and the lush domestic acres of cottages and manor house alike. Plum and cherry, both wild and domestic, hawthorn and blackthorn, spiraea and elder – all it seems signalling summer with their scented prophecies. A yaffle (green woodpecker) laughs as it flies from the nearby woods and settles in an ash tree by the river in Ulting churchyard. The shingles on the church spire are riddled with holes – evidence of regular visits by this drumming denizen of woods and large mature gardens. I've seen tree-creepers and nuthatches in this particular graveyard – and even a skulking blackcap on just one, ever so memorable occasion!

St George's Day is upon us and the cuckoo's double note rings its hollow distant bell across meadows thick with primroses and cowslips. It is Shakespeare's birthday: 'Where the bee sucks there suck I, in a cowslip's ear I lie, merrily, merrily'. It is said that he also died on this very day! But no-one dies because no-one is ever born, we've always been here, always will be – it's true; believe me. This is a dream my friends; and illusion, a glorious illusion. Enjoy the dream while you can, but remember, reality is elsewhere: as Plato once so wisely said – 'we are like people living in a cave, believing the flickering shadows on the wall to be all there is of truth'. It is not so my friends, not so; the summerlands await you – you've been there before many times and you will certainly return. You can live this earthly dream for an eternity if you wish, or else you can evolve whenever you are ready and travel to the higher realms of your infinite spiritual being: 'As above, so below'; 'Eternity in a grain of sand', as Blake so profoundly postulated. Jack-by-the-Hedge (hedge garlic) picks the flickering orange-tip butterflies from the precincts of the sun-enlightened hedgerows, sweet violets peep from the shadows like diminutive purple emperors and the fields of oilseed rape burst into flower like a vernal fire. Gold and blue: golden clouds, golden fields, blue sky and the first few bluebells in the woods – what could be more perfect than this; more holy and hallowed and revered?

The land between Chelmsford and Maldon is intensively farmed. It is an area of very mixed agricultural production. Wheat, barley (a crop that Essex is justly famous for) and rape tend to be grown on the drier slopes, while potatoes and sugar beet can be seen on heavier land closer to the river. Sheep are no where near as prolific as they used to be but cattle still graze the flood meadows and there are larger more intensively farmed dairy units across the A12 beyond Hatfield Peverel. One of the driest parts of England falls within a triangle formed by Marks Tey, Maldon and Chelmsford and as a consequence of this top fruits are favoured crops in the area: Blackcurrants, redcurrants, gooseberries, strawberries, etc……. Most of them are grown in locations like Tiptree between Maldon and Colchester but a number of top fruit growers are found further south and west towards the Chelmsford area. The dry conditions also make for good seed growing conditions, most of this is also carried out further to the north in places like Coggelshall but much seed is produced to the west of Maldon and in fact most English grown seed comes from places within the aforementioned Essex triangle. There is some poultry and pig farming in the immediate vicinity of the navigation and occasionally one sees more unusual crops such as, borage or flax. When I worked for the aerial crop sprayers I once saw a large acreage of poppies being grown for the pharmaceutical industry in the Wickham Bishops area and peas and especially beans with their beautiful flowers are not that uncommon.

As inevitably as the cycle of the seasons and the crops Easter comes round again: Easter, named it's said after the Pagan Goddess – Eostre – Goddess of the dawn. A movable feast, Christian and yet determined by the phases of the moon. Easter Sunday is the first Sunday after the Paschal full moon – the full moon that occurs on the spring equinox or any of the following 28 days. Therefore Easter Sunday cannot be earlier than March the 22nd or later than April the 25th. It was often said that the sun danced on Easter Day – and why not I ask, why not indeed? It is Easter Bank Holiday Monday and I drive down to one of the most beautiful and interesting churches in the area – St Mary the Virgin at Little Baddow. The church is set just north of the village in a typically English country lane. Lilac and laburnum are a riot of blue, white, lilac and gold in the cottage gardens and the thrushes and blackbirds are singing their strident anthems to the risen Lord. The church surrounded by trees to the south and east looks out across farmland to the river below Boreham. There is a Norman doorway in the north wall but the church was obviously widened at sometime in the 14th century when the west tower was built and windows installed. Inside there are two recesses with two beautifully carved oak effigies – c1330 – of a man and a woman lying on tomb chests. Today the building is highly decorated; gone are the glooms of Lent, the purple drapes have been removed from the statuary and the brass-work and the crosses are all gleaming resplendently. There is a model representation of the tomb or 'cave' from which Christ resurrected and garlands of 'palm' (pussy willow) are as thick and sweet as honey between the candles and the pews. In the chancel there is a spectacular monument to Sir Henry Mildmay 1639, who lived at Graces in the parish. One of the former ladies of the house is said to have committed suicide and apparently can still be seen walking her ghostly way along the country pathway that is now known as 'Graces walk' at the southern end of the parish! Some 14th century stained-glass can still be seen in the east window (a rarity after the sickening despoilation of the churches committed by evangelical puritans) and a medieval wall painting of St Christopher c1375. Recently work from the 12th century has been uncovered including: a depiction of the Devil and some 13th century double line masonry patterns. I make my way outside through the primroses the daffodils and the early tulips; and in the north facing graveyard an amelanchier is in full magnificent bloom. Greenfinches wheeze, skylarks soar on the edge of their lifting songs, and the sunlight dazzles from the depths of a cache of sapphires. There is a wild flower garden devoted entirely to species of plants associated with the Blessed Virgin Mary either in folklore or legend and I remember my childhood days with the rosary and thoughts of the 'Mystical Rose' return to haunt me. The sun may dance at Easter but winter is not yet finished with whiteness and the words of the silent snow.

A 'blackthorn winter'; a wise old saw from the past – when the blackthorn's in bloom towards the end of April the wind may yet turn into the north or the east and give us one last unwholesome blast from the frozen precincts of Boreas. Not just snow, but frost that nips the fruit buds and the flowers, and gives the horticulturalist many a sleepless night. When everything is lush and looking green a pall of belated whiteness is unwelcome to say the least. I love the snow in its due season but today at the end of April the swirling flakes sadden me beyond belief. Give me the thrush and the blackbird and the swallow, not the vast and empty silences of snow. Give me the kaleidoscope of country garden flowers not the uniformity of whiteness and a pewter sky. Give me warmth and Jack-by-the-Hedge not old Jack Frost freezing the twilight with his breath of steel. I am longing for the 'Green Man' to finally break the bonds of an iron winter as he looks from the bosses of our ancient churches and breathes the breath of foliage and flowers. The snow will not last, these 'blackthorn winters' are always short lived. May Day is on the horizon and Bel the sky God is already working on the freshly fallen snow. Boreas will inevitably have to retreat to his northern castle of ice and the oak and the hawthorn will trample the facets of the glint and melting crystals.

Bluebell woods – Little Baddow

Amelanchier – St Mary the Virgin – Little Baddow

Beeleigh weir and lock

St Mary the Virgin – Little Baddow

Late snow - Ulting

Early Spring - Ulting

Little Baddow Hall

Woodham Walter

MAY
POEMS:

RIVER ALBUM

We know this place –
Have made it something special.

We trace the seasons through the camera's eye –
Make images, mechanical with light,
To frame our thoughts, like memories in aspic.

Just you and I, and the river's cold transparency:
The negatives of ever-changing sky
Sliding beneath us on the edge of focus –

The deep, deceptive spirit of our lives;
Doubled and distant, like a slow exposure.

MAY THE FIFTH

The arrival of the swifts –
For days I've watched,
Nothing:
And yet there they are,
Five on the evening air –
Curved into substance
By the thought of summer.

Cuneiform on blue papyrus –
Fluent with contrast:
All night they'll fly –
Ink to the sky's ink,
Lost to the liquid
Of the leaching stars.

Tomorrow,
When the flowers wake –
When the words of fragrance
Climb on the voices
Of the warming earth:
They'll underline
The languages they make –
Screech over paper,
Like a nib that scratches.

TULIPS

Somehow, they scream –
Silent of course,
Like a dream in scarlet.

Flowers shouldn't frighten,
But they do –
Row upon row of muted shock,
Filling the garden with a sense of panic.

The bees are not perturbed –
Laborious, on loud, vibrating wings,
They turn their thoughts to deep communications.

They enter in as fearlessly as light –
As if a far and disembodied voice
Had found the chords to pollinate its language.

May Day or Beltaine – take your choice. Bel, the sky God and the Welsh (tan) meaning fire. The young Stag Lord represents the God and the maiden or May Queen equates with the Goddess. When the Stag Lord overcomes his antlered adversary he will take the hand of the May Queen and the land's fertility will be assured. Or is it the Holly and the Oak Lord who fight for the hand of the maiden? The oak is associated with thunder and the pulls on window blinds always used to be carved in the shape of an acorn for protection against the elements. The Holly Lord always loses the battle at Beltaine and retreats to the woods with his wild hounds until Samhaine; meanwhile the Oak Lord marries the May Queen and 'All's right with the world'. The hawthorn - or may tree - was the symbol of the season of sexual fun and games throughout Europe before the Reformation. This of course upset the prudish Christians and ever since the may tree has been considered unlucky, as is the month of May for marriages! The mayflies dance by the bridge at Paper Mills lock. They moult twice; once from the larval stage to become duns, and then again as flying insects when metamorphosis turns them into resplendent, glistening spinners. Short-lived ephemera they mate in shimmering swarms above the river, are readily eaten by fish and marauding birds, and the females that survive lay their eggs on the water under the moon and suddenly expire. Sad, but eminently sensible; the food chain has been furnished – 'God works in mysterious ways'! The riverside meadows are thick with buttercups; the oilseed rape is in full flower, sweet scented, and heavy with cumbersome bees. The world is gold against blue – a paradisal contrast, sublime. Across the flowering rape the first returning swifts hawk for flies on scything, sickle wings and a nightingale sings its diurnal song from the billowing blooms of the equally scented may. In Blake's Wood, south of Little Baddow, sorrel and anemones, stitchwort and campion, welcome the glorious bluebells – England's major claim to fame in my opinion. A yaffle laughs and the striated sunlight sifts through the branches of the trees and gilds a blue and perfect nether sky. The great-tits double ring echoes from every corner of the wood and the spirit of summer shimmers in mirages from the surrounding fields. Zephyr, God of the west wind, fell in love with Anemone; his wife Flora (Goddess of the spring) became so jealous that he was forced to abandon her. Boreas (God of the north wind) courted her and in return she flowered for him every May. In the Middle Ages sap from the bluebell was used as a gum to fix feathers to the shafts of arrows – 'all's fair in love and war' it seems! Greater and lesser spotted woodpeckers drum on the distant trees and an occasional flash of black and red and white flares and dazzles as they dart between the shadows. The jays are exceedingly raucous. The most exotic members of the crow family they seem almost out of place, incongruous, in pink and white and pale-perfected blue. On the edge of the woods, kestrels hover and sparrow hawks quarter the field. Skylarks climb to a vanishing point; a pencil point, a full stop to their own far-flung cadenzas. Pairs of cabbage whites convolve in lifting spirals, settle their territorial disputes and then separate into whispered, white soliloquies. May, what a glorious golden month, caught on the cusp between spring and summer. Its gemstone is emerald and its flower the may. Grass and corn and cabbage whites; growth and purity, love and fertility – what more could we ask for? The Anglo Saxons named the month *tri milchi* because the grazing was so good that cows could be milked three times a day. The Rogation Days fall in May when the *beating of the bounds* takes place around the parish and the clergy pray for an exceptional harvest. The Thursday after Rogation Sunday is Ascension Day. Skylarks with gold on their wings are an image of Christ ascending into heaven and the world seems prelapsarian. May dew has been collected and the ladies bathe their faces as they dream of eternal beauty. Enough of the woods and the fields and the may-flowering thorn, I must drive back down to the river and renew my acquaintance with the mayflies and the rising dace.

Paper Mills comes to life in May. People are busy working on their boats and barges and the tea room (run by the wonderfully warm and friendly Susie Clift) serves refreshments as and when the mariners and passing trade require them. The lock opens and closes and another craft passes on its way from Chelmsford to Heybridge Basin and back. I can hear the rooks somewhere near Little Baddow Hall and lapwings fly over 'Rainbirds' – a house named after them. Danbury hill rises above us, at some 365 ft above sea level – one of the highest points in Essex. A party of tourists have boarded 'Victoria', a traditionally painted canal barge, for a trip through Rushes lock and on to the lush surroundings of Ulting's ancient Church. Across from the lock at Paper Mills is the tiny red brick 'bothy' where the bargees would spend the night, while their horses were stabled in what is now the Old Stables Tea Room. There are also moorings at Heybridge Basin both for sea and land based craft, at Hoe Mill in the lock cut, at Sandford cut and in Chelsmford itself. The canal offers 14 miles of rural charm for ramblers, boating types and anglers and here at Paper Mills I am at the heart of this water borne paradise. Willow warblers sing from the ubiquitous cricket bat willows and their green-cum-silver feathery leaves cast cool reflections in the rippling mill pool. A pike holds station behind one of the bridge's buttresses and a shoal of unwary roach swim perilously close to danger. Nature, 'red in tooth and claw' they say; where there is pleasure there is pain, where there is calm there is storm, where there is love there is hate! Duality – it's inevitable; you can't have one thing without its opposite – that is reality as we know it – temporal truth. But you can transcend the dilemma as I do now standing on this bridge. Look into the river, deep into your double self, your spiritual alter image. Fish will swim between you and the reflected clouds and you will know that you inhabit two worlds simultaneously. Spirit and material, body and soul, heaven and earth: A willow warbler's sweet unearthly cadence fathoms the warming air and a green and golden lily bursts at its watery bud. Is this a dream or reality – reality or a dream – who knows? I thank the Gods of all religions; Pagan, Christian, or otherwise. The May month gathers its garlands as it comes towards its end and the screeching swifts and twittering swallows break the spell that's held me rapt for hours.

In the late 1960's the wildlife along the Chelmer was decimated by chemical pollution: herbicides, insecticides and PCB's being among the worst substances. The food chain was affected to such an extent that both fish-eating and land-dwelling birds were unable to breed as their egg shells became too thin to be viable. Mammals suffered a similar fate as they were being slowly poisoned to death and the previous incalculable numbers of insects dropped to alarming levels. To add insult to injury we'd already suffered the ravages of myxomatosis and Dutch Elm disease and to increase agricultural productivity even more, institutional farmers were ploughing the fields right up to the edge and not allowing for any headland to be left wild – the perfect habitat for 'weeds', insects and the pheasant and partridge chicks that fed on them. Nowadays things have improved greatly; there are still the problems of oestrogen, detergents, water abstraction and too much nitrogen from fertilisers seeping into the river, but all in all things are looking better than they've done for decades. Pheasant and partridge – both red-legged and English – are back in abundance and the headlands are rich with wild geraniums, herb Robert, sow thistles, mayweed, meadowsweet and much, much more. Along the river itself, in addition to the indigenous heron, beautiful white little Egrets have started to colonise the waterways and wet pastures. Mute swans there are in plenty and the fish-eating great crested grebe rises from the water in spring to amaze the onlooker with its intricate courtship ritual. The blue-skied and orange sunset flash of the kingfisher can be seen as it darts like a biological missile over the river's glittering surface and the moorhens and coots that are with us all through the year are augmented in summer by their visiting European cousins. After many years of being extinct in Essex otters have made a welcome return to the Chelmer and Blackwater Navigation and deer and badgers come down to drink the sweet and wholesome waters at dawn and dusk all the way from the surrounding woodlands. Fish that were becoming scarce and hard to catch are back in increasing numbers: perch, recovered from the disease that decimated them nationwide, roach, dace, bream, chub, pike, the occasional river carp, rudd and the odd brown trout, are all now thriving in the relatively unpolluted waters. The cricket bat willows also thrive in the damp conditions along the river and are thus not only valuable as a crop but also protect the river-banks from erosion. These trees are felled about every 15 years and a 'set' – a long willow pole cut from another tree is planted to replace them. Up to a few years ago there were osier beds along by Ulting Lane, grown and cut for basket making and such like, and the beautiful purples of their stems were the perfect

71

contrast to the shadowy swamps they inhabited. As an added bonus, in spring, the marshy areas by the willow stands and osier beds were thick with the magnificent blooms of marsh marigolds – May blobs or kingcups to the countryman. Metallic demoiselles and gauzy winged dragonflies (the Devil's darning needles) flutter and dart across the river all summer long and hornets chew on alder wood and ash to make their nests when the summer sun sizzles in the hot transpiring leaves. Dusk is coming on and although it's said "don't cast a clout 'til May is out' the weather is exceptionally warm and the sun as it sets over the navigation is a round, recumbent, distended ball of ruby fire, a perfect accompaniment to the blackbirds' and the thrushes' twilight songs. June is around the next meander of the river and the all-night flying swifts climb ever higher until it seems they will be able to reach out and touch the 'heavenly twins' – Castor and Pollux.

Author fishing near Hoe Mill

Typical Chelmer scene

Springfield wharf

Road bridge – Paper Mills

74

'Rainbirds' – near Paper Mills

The Cricketer's Arms – Danbury Common

SPELL

That evening in June, when we walked the river;
The moon, exactly halved –
A ghost at the zenith while the sun still lingered.

We two, amongst the comfrey and the mallow,
Talking in whispers, like the trees above us.

Was it the anglers who encouraged us to silence,
Or the thought that something other –
Some startled bird or levitating fish
Might break the spell and shatter our reflections?

I only know that fallow field was best:
The mayweed and the poppies unresolved –
Their colours blent of innocence and passion.

To see you there, through shadows dressed with gold,
Diffuse, as if evolving from a dream;
Was something told that I cannot forget –
Will yet redeem when light has lost its swallows.

HEAVENWARDS

There's not much grace
When a swan takes wing –
What with faith
And gravity in opposition
And the skin of water
Losing its tension
To the webbed assault;

It's hard to think
Of anything like finesse,
When every thought
Has laughter as its link
To test the bonds
Of beauty and deportment;

But when it springs
Long-headed into flight,
Beyond the walk
Absurdly over waves,
It brings to earth
An aspect of delight
That names itself
The element of angels.

WEIRPOOL

The wind through aspens
Echoes the river as it leaps the weir.

A wagtail's yellow flicker doubles
With sunlight through the plumes of spray –
Worries the spectrum into shifts of focus.

Nettles and cleavers sharpen
Their incense on the edge of silt –
Spatter the clothing with their green stigmata.

A chub noses into light,
Then buries its own gold.

Irreligious coots shatter
The icons of intense reflection –
Bicker, like sceptics, in a shrine of rushes.

June, and the dog roses constellate in the hedgerows like stars immersed in strawberries and cream. Damsel flies bring high summer down to earth and the river on their red, green and blue, glittering metallic bodies. Reed warblers chirr in the bank-side rushes and the golden chalices of the newly opened water lilies are lifted on green-outstretching palms to catch the honeyed liquors of the sun. The fishing season has opened again and I cross the bridge south of Bumfords Lane and walk east along the towpath towards Rushes lock. My tackle is heavy, but it will be well worth the effort when I eventually get there. Rushes lock, where the River Ter and the navigation meet. So isolated and between the roads at Paper Mills and Hoe Mill, that all I will see today will be the cattle and the wildlife, the occasional rambler, an angler or two perhaps and the odd barge, cruiser or canoeist.

This is without doubt the closest to heaven on earth that you're ever likely to come across anywhere in England. It is quintessentially English: A meandering river, cattle meadows, dusky summer trees, a church spire in the leafy distance, lark song and a profusion of wild flowers and humming bees. I can feel the heat reaching to my very bones. Ring and collared doves accentuate the warmth with their deep syllabic cooing and a yellow wagtail flickers across to its nest in the crumbling brickwork by the edge of the weir. Shall I fish above the weir in the deeper, slowest water, in the weir pool itself, or under the alders in the chub-haunted back stream? It doesn't matter, the sun is high in the sky, the yellowhammers are singing their long drawn our songs: 'a little bit of bread and no cheese.........' and the corn buntings are jangling their vocal keys over the ripening corn. Will it be tench or roach or chub? Why worry, each is as good as the other. I put a large perch float on the line and attach a number twelve hook; drag it through the silkweed on the weir and cast into the racing white-entrancing waters of the pool. The careering float stops for an instant and I strike and a prime, perfected, pink-bellied, river smelling roach of about 2lbs comes thrashing through the crystal spray to my waiting net. Roach, the epitome of river fishing, a boy's recurring dream, a man's hard earned reality. Have you ever smelt a roach; they are the crux of everything rivery - the archetypical fish of the angler's collective unconscious. I catch a few more roach, some smaller and some larger, and decide to go to the back stream to fish for the elusive chub. I freeline bread flake under the overhanging alders and a monstrous rubber-lipped denizen of the tree roots rises to take the bait. It's on and it pumps and plunges to abysmal depths taking the test curve of my rod to its limits. The fight is hard but short-lived and I soon have it beaten. It is the crock of gold at the end of my piscatorial rainbow – a glint-scaled, aureate miracle! All I need now is a tench or a bream from above the weir and my day will be well and truly complete. I lay on deep with a bunch of lob worms. The float lifts, lies flat and then sails away between the lily-pads: a beautiful bronze bream of nearly 3lbs runs a few times before I turn its head and draw it on its flank across the water's surface to the landing net. I cast again; the float dips once, twice, three times and then disappears. This time the fight is different, the clutch screams as line is taken off the reel, and the fish heads for the rushes and freedom. I apply side-strain and regain control of the battle. This fish will not give up, it dives and runs time and time again and seems like it will never tire. But it does and I have it beaten – a red-eyed, olive-sided, wondrous 4lb tench – my day's complete; my patience has been rewarded.

The sun has reached its zenith and there are two festivals to celebrate – the Summer solstice and Midsummer's Day. From now on the days will get shorter but this will be compensated for by an increase in heat during July and August. Modern day Druids will be waiting for the sunrise at Stonhenge, but Stonehenge was probably as much a moon and star temple where the movement of the heavenly bodies was observed. The larger stone circles at Avebury are probably where the Old Ones worshipped the sun and is a far more important site for discerning Pagans. It is a time for casting spells: Shakespeare's '*A midsummer Night's Dream*' had a speech about fairies and Puck (the Old One) according to Kipling is hereabouts I'm sure by the River Chelmer. Shakespeare's plays were full of spells and magic. The famous spells made by the *Three Witches in Macbeth* sound somewhat gruesome but in fact are rather different when you understand the reasoning behind them. They are in fact to do with the country names of herbs: *Jew's liver* is the Jew's ear fungus, *grease from the murderer's gibbet* is bittersweet, hairy mullein was known as *wool of bat, eye of newt* – rocket, *gall of goat* – goat's rue and *tongue of dog* undoubtedly hound's tongue! On Midsummer Day we should decorate our houses with birch twigs and rose, but it's considered to be very unlucky to hear a cuckoo calling on the festival day itself! The gemstone for June is either pearl or moonstone and both seem particularly suited to the season. Pale blue skies and the wild and cultivated roses, such as 'iceberg'; ameliorate the sun's increasing heat with their cooling colours and the moon at dusk is like a pearl set against the bluest velvet. Flowers of the month are the rose and the honeysuckle and I for one am both captured and enraptured by their inimitable fragrances. June is the most prolific time for the rose, especially the red rose; symbol of love – of England and St George. The cottage gardens along and around the Chelmer and its valley are no exception to the rule. From Danbury to Little Baddow, Ulting to Hoe Mill and on to Woodham Walter, from Sandford lock to Barnes Mill and from Beeleigh to Heybridge Basin, roses of every imaginable hue and form entrance the senses with their sweet and kaleidoscopic displays. Honeysuckle, as well, covers the trellis and the privet hedge in many an isolated country garden and its unbelievable bee-enchanting scent pervades all the lanes and byways of Midsummer.

It's time to walk from Hoe Mill bridge to Ricketts lock before the heat becomes too intense and the spirit begins to weaken. A flotilla of swans and signets float with the gentle flow towards the wide bend close to the wooden footbridge and Ulting Lane. The hay has been cut in the waterside meadows and the scent is both delightful and delirious. Comfrey almost obliterates the towpath with its white, blue and many-purpled bells, and the bees are heavy with nectar and pollen and the laborious drone of a hot midsummer's noon. Amphibious bistort lifts its pink plumes into the rising heat and the perspiring loosestrife dowses its purples into deep and cool reflections. Mallow in great mauve swathes picks commas and painted ladies from the air by the riverside cottages and swifts and swallows fly beneath the water main and out across the cattle-grazing meadows. Mallards with ducklings, like powder puffs, in tow, dabble in the shallows for cabbage weed and other tasty water borne delights. I come to the 200 year old brick-built bridge at Ricketts lock and lean across the parapet looking westwards. Farmland and riverine willows lead my eyes towards the slopes of Danbury Ridge, the woodlands and the isolated houses. I turn into the east and a spinney stretches towards Beeleigh lock and falls, and beyond the 'Long Pond' travels to Heybridge Basin, Collier's Reach and the Blackwater Estuary. My mind is racing to all points of the compass at once and I feel as though I am everywhere I see simultaneously. Time and place seem to have been eclipsed. I am an integral part of the whole of my formative landscape. I am the geology, the sub-soil and the tilth. History doesn't exist, everything's happening now – right now. I keep turning around on the bridge; Maldon and Chelmsford, Hatfield Peverel and Woodham Mortimer are all merging into one and light is becoming as bright and intense as the heat. A White Canon from Beeleigh Abbey holds me by the shoulders and haunts me with his ghostly plainsong. A spectral white horse is drawing a barge of timber along the towpath in my mind's incongruous eye and a group of navvies drink small-beer as they munch on chunks of bread and cheese and raw onion. Grace's Walk is haunted by a sad and desolate maiden of the 'past' and Sir Henry Mildmay drifts transparently across from St Mary the Virgin by Little Baddow Hall to parley with the ghostly Earls of Essex on the banks of the river at Beeleigh. Is this a dream or is it reality? The river is clear, as clear as a crystal ball, and I scry beneath the surface for the truth. 'Truth, what is truth - jested Pilot? Am I a poet or a madman – a fool or a wise man – who knows? Slowly my everyday senses return and I watch as a water vole cuts vees across the river. How has it managed to survive the ravages of the feral mink, the competition for food from the ubiquitous brown rat? Rabbits are cropping grass in the shadows at the edge of a hawthorn thicket and a fox looks on with a long and drooling tongue. June is nearly at an end: how many Junes have I stood here on this bridge; can they be numbered or are they numberless - timeless even? Swifts and swallows fly beneath the bridge as if their wings were oiled – silent and summery in the slant of the evening light. Thoughts are again of home –

wherever home is! I retrace my steps past the water main, the cottages, the wooden footbridge and the wide bend in the river. A thrush repeats its clear and crystal notes from a tall oak. A heron glides across low in the sky and croaks like an out of tune motor horn. Hoe Mill comes into view and a few people in shirt sleeves are taking advantage of the calm and mild dusk. Lights are going on in the lock keepers cottage and the boats moored in the cut. A tawny owl hoots eerily and the evening star (venus) scratches the river's glass. I settle back in my car, light my pipe, and start the engine. The spell is broken – time reasserts itself. I turn the lane by Hoe Farm and a hare stands transfixed in the beam of my headlights. Sacred to the moon – to Diana the Huntress: I stop, turn off my lights, leave it for a few seconds and then turn them on again. The hare has gone – completely disappeared; dematerialised. Was it real, that silver apparition in the night, or was it all in my imagination – who knows? I drive through Woodham Walter and the moon above the church spire is full and round and resonant of night as it beats like a soundless drum inside my heart. July will come with more of the same heat – more of the same time and more of its seeming timelessness. Bickenacre Priory is cloistered by the deep, enveloping velvet of the darkness and a far off Woodham Ferrers reaches through the sunset for the stars.

Spring tide – below the weir at Beeleigh

The 'Long Pond' and Maldon golf club

Summer flowers near Hoe Mill

Cow parsley – Ulting church

Eve's Corner - Danbury

Sugar Mill cottages – Ulting Lane

METAMORPHOSES

We camped beside the river. The ring-doves
Linked their syllables of sound and summer

Drowsed in heat. We fished with wheat and hemp
And tried with all our callow skill, to tempt

The silver seams. The river spun its glass
With every breeze. A glancing light that passed

From wave to wave and left us in a trance
We half believed. The damsel-flies, enhanced

The balmy air. Their glint metallic wings,
Diaphanous as dreams. Our pleasure hinged

On goose-quills tipped with paint. Each subtle dip
Would flex the waiting hand and lock its grip

On sub-aquatic treasure. At dusk the moon
Would rise behind the ash, a gold doubloon

Suspended in the calm, as herons crashed
Ungainly to their roost. The stars were cash

In heaven's open purse and pipistrelles
Converged on tracks of sound, to ring the knell

Of many hapless moths. The 'Tilley Lamps'
Were lit, and in the grass the dews of damp

Condensed. The tawny owls conversed. Two ghosts
That rose to our deluded ears and closed

The final chapter of the day. We went
To makeshift beds – cocooned within the tent –

Where every silken syllable of light
Dissolved before our metamorphic eyes.

BIRDWATCHING

I watched a warbler hawking butterflies –
Hovering, like a kestrel, by the loosestrife.

A cuckoo, several times the warbler's size,
Waited with a wide gape
For fresh supplies of cabbage-whites and commas.

Next year, when spring with double-note surprise
Awakens thoughts of summer fields and flowers,
I'll think again how beauty paid the price –
How paradise was fed on angel's wings.

THE ESOTERIC ANGLER

He knew the river well –
Was fluent with its meanings.

Though asked to tell,
His answers were evasive –

Kept to the margins,
Like a shoal of secrets.

Equivocation was his lure –
Meanderings, his disposition.

No-one for sure
Could penetrate the depths –

Fathom the contents
In his mesh of words.

Once hooked, and held secure,
He waited till you leapt

Towards the light. Then slowly,
With a deftness that procures,

He drew you in,
And ministered the priest.

Priest: blunt instrument used for despatching fish.

The Dog-star (Sirius) rises with the sun and doubles the heat of
July – or so the Romans once said! Ring-doves (wood pigeons)

and collared-doves add to the rising warmth with their hollow summer sounds. As the day moves inexorably towards its zenith, yellowhammers and corn buntings serenade the newly gilded wheat and barley. Crickets and grasshoppers stridulate; rasp their monotonous love songs from the hedgerows and the meadow grasses. Reed and sedge warblers chirr and across the river from Ulting church mirages add new and shimmering lakes to the burning pastures. In the bushes beside the canal a cuckoo chick – the size of an inflated football – is being fed butterflies by a tiny warbler – life is definitely stranger than fiction! It's too hot for fishing – nothing is feeding except the cuckoo chick. I doze by the river and the mackerel sky coruscates in white and gold. Most of the birds have ceased their singing and all is the rasp and drone of insects and the doves' incessant syllables. This is what we dream of in December. A hot-air balloon drifts across from Danbury Ridge uncannily – as incongruous as Concorde; out of place and out of time. The barge Victoria cuts a white swathe through the water and the thud of its engine adds to the sense of unreality. I drift in and out of sleep and the purples of the delving loosestrife are somehow suspect and surreal. This cannot be true – surely there is no paradise on earth – surely? I may be drifting in and out of sleep but this is no dream: perhaps not the wider eternal reality, but a temporal signature, a sign, an outward expression of spiritual grace. 'In the beginning there was the word, and then there was light'. Light is all there is – I am a being of light – everything is illuminant and enlightened. Can it last – can the transcended present maintain its delirious hold on my imagination? I may be centred on indolence but the old adage 'those that wive 'twixt sickle and scythe shall never thrive' shows that others are hard at work in this busiest of farming seasons. There is little time between haymaking and harvest for affairs of the heart – the crops are far more important. Larkspur and delphiniums powder their blues in the cottage gardens and hollyhocks and sunflowers climb towards the hot and lark-less skies. Close to the source of both the rivers Chelmer and Blackwater lies Dunmow. July is the month of 'The Dunmow Flitch' when if a married couple can prove to the appointed judges that they have 'not wished themselves unmarried for twelvemonth and a day' they win a flitch of bacon. It is said that this quaint old ceremony goes back as far as the 12th century.

July the 15th and it rains again at last. This is St Swithin's Day – will the prophecy come true; will it rain for forty days and forty nights? Probably not – thank goodness. This is warm summer rain, the sort that lays the dust and scents the air with sweetness. The birds are encouraged to sing again and the blackbird and the thrush add to the sparkle of the glittering droplets in the branches. The air's still warm but fresher, less humid. People are out and about again – their siestas forgotten. Fishermen cast into the fish-enlivened waters and catch, or nearly catch their dreams! Ramblers ramble and boating types undo their mooring ropes and head for their own re-enactments of 'Swallows and Amazons'. Toad of Toad Hall, Badger and Ratty and Mole make their nostalgic way beneath the blue-be-silvered willows and the callow dreams of Charles Kingsley swim ever youthful with the sinuous shoals of shimmering roach. The grass is steaming in warmth, like the ghostly spirit of the soil searching for sunlight and the world of vision. Darkness has found the light and a corn bunting, like a diminutive St Peter, dangles the keys of heaven with its song. Convolvulus opens its Gabriel's horns and a mass of angelic bees enter to receive God's honeyed and eternal messages. All is Annunciation – everything is impregnated with the thoughts of deity – the word is manifest. Water nymphs comb the golden hair of lilies in the river. Dryads whisper from the far from weeping willows, and a goat-footed Pan, pipes with the warbler and the skulking blackcap. My memory takes me back to another summer, long ago in my youth, my early teenage years. My mind travels from Beeleigh, under the old brick bridge, and over the Long Pond all the way to Heybridge Basin –

to the ancient quayside inn, the Dutch eel barges, the wide sea lock and Collier's reach on the Blackwater Estuary.

When Maldon was bypassed by the canal because of local opposition Heybridge Basin grew in proportion to its new-found importance. A small port was built and the sea lock was able to accommodate vessels up to 300 tons in weight. The navigation itself could handle lighters up to 60 feet in length with a payload of about 60 tons. Larger vessels were off-loaded into barges off Norsey Island in the Blackwater and their cargoes transferred to the lighters in the canal for transportation to Chelmsford. The onetime ubiquitous Thames barges (spritsail barges) were also regular visitors to the Basin with their cargoes of corn, hay, straw and clay for brick making. Designed for shoal waters they were also useful for taking goods right up the shallow creeks where other vessels dare not venture. In olden times fishing was a very important activity in the area. Herrings, sprats, sole, cod and plaice were all caught in large numbers by the inshore fishing craft. Oysters were important as well and still are further along the estuary in such places as Mersea Island and Brightlingsea on the River Colne. My own particular memories concern those Dutch eel barges in those long ago hot summers of my youth. We used to watch the men transferring the eels in long-handled nets from the larger craft into the smaller water-filled lighters for their journey to Chelmsford and beyond. Inevitably many of the eels were lost overboard and greatly increased the already considerable stocks roaming the canal. These we would fish for regularly – not just for fun; although that was part of it – but for money! We had our own market for lives eels and even in those far off days they held a very good price indeed. We would arrive at the canal in the late afternoon with rods and lines and an assortment of containers to hold our catch. We nearly always fished at night – eels and hot, sultry summer nights are almost synonymous. The moon would rise from the Blackwater Estuary like a gold doubloon and stars would stipple and scintillate on the river's surface. Lob worms or maggots, it didn't matter. When eels are ravenous you don't have to wait long for a bite. Eels have a strange life history. They migrate as elvers all the way from the Sargasso Sea in the Caribbean, stay for a couple of years until they reach sexual maturity and then travel all the way back to breed. Why – don't ask me – I'm no marine biologist! It is also said that those eels that remain sterile never return to the spawning grounds and grow to inordinate, terrifying sizes as can be vouched for by any eel-fishing specimen hunter. We always caught enough to keep us happy – to fill our ever-empty juvenile coffers. I remember once in the early hours of one warm summer's morning, feeling a certain wriggling sensation in my mouth as I was eating my sandwiches. Maggots had escaped into my lunchbox and I was unwarily munching my way through a handful of the wriggling little critters! Not to worry, I reasoned, eels eat maggots and I eat eels, so what's the difference? In fact they didn't really taste that bad – honestly! In those days there was a regular traffic in timber for Brown and Sons in Chelmsford carried out by large metal barges with out-board motors at the stern. Those particular barges carried on working right up to the early 1970's and did a marvellous job of keeping the river weed in check. If I remember rightly, when I fished at places like Hoe Mill, Ulting and Paper Mills, they went up to Chelmsford and back once a day and there was always a friendly wave or a passing of the time of day with the bargees. Nowadays, Heybridge Basin is used almost entirely by pleasure craft, but for me personally it's none the worse for that. What with the two pubs by the Basin and the Mill Beach Hotel just to the north on the edge of the Blackwater the place is as near perfect as it's ever been. You still see the occasional larger sailing vessel or a renovated Thames barge or two moored up along the canal's banks and holidaymakers, fishermen, ramblers and yachtsmen all take advantage of the peace and sea-aired tranquillity it has to offer.

I decide to go for a drive along the many lanes that border the Navigation. Now that the headlands are back and flowering profusely, partridge and pheasant are as prolific as they've ever been. Mayweed and harebells vie for ascendancy with such other beautiful plants as: cranesbills, herb Robert, poppies and mallow. Lanes either side of the canal all the way from Maldon to Boreham are equally delightful. I stop in Tofts Chase, half way up to the top of Danbury Ridge, get out of the car, and stand at the edge of a field overlooking the distant river. It is still and hot and very humid – I'm perspiring and somewhat uncomfortable. I move under the shade of an oak, sit down and rest my back against its trunk. The weather is perfect for one of the seasonal wonders of nature – flying ants. Stillness, humidity and heat, ideal conditions for creating thermals, ideal conditions for the insects' far dispersals. Thousands of them seem to gain their gauzy wings simultaneously – perhaps millions! They rise on the thermals high into the warm and lactic blue of a summer sky. The swifts and swallows and seagulls are ready and waiting for them. They know it is their time of plenty – welcome abundance in a parched, near drought-ridden land. Nature always produces far more than it needs, as if death is purely incidental. Something dies that something else may live – that is the way of the world, like it or not. But it doesn't diminish the spectacle; the clouds of clamouring birds, the seeming mist of insects. A weasel, like a cigar tube on legs, scurries across the road with something warm and furry in its mouth. A slowworm follows the same route and is attacked by a missel thrush. It sheds the tip of its tail, the thrush is taken aback, startled by the writhing, incongruous entity, and the slowworm escapes to breed again. The thrush's chicks are desperate for food; the weather has been too good; there are far too many mouths to feed. Crows and magpies take advantage of the small deaths, the rabbit and pheasant flattened on the road, the chick ejected from its nest. The meadowsweet is thick with 'seeds' – or is it? No, they are pollen beetles, thousands of them – nature's over abundance once again. The verges are lush with umbellifers: hogweed and hemlock, wild carrot and fennel. The cow parsley vanished along with spring and early summer but the umbels of this varied and difficult to identify family of plants still offer a haven for numerous insects. The ladybird – each different species recognised by the number of spots – grazes in the snow-like meadows of the musky scented flowers. Soldier beetles munch until disturbed and then show themselves as far more aerial than most of their kith and kin. On the hard clay – cracked to chasms buy the July heat – an adder lies coiled in the sun and on a nearby anthill a common lizard gorges on eggs and ants in equal measure. I drive back down to the river beside Ulting church, look for some summer shade beneath the trees and sleep for the rest of the afternoon and most of the sultry evening. I'm awoken by a pair of tawny owls; tu whit says one, tu whoo says the other. For the first time in many years I hear the nightjar again – the churn owl; the goat sucker. Its continuous cicada-like song adds a Mediterranean dimension to the gently rolling Essex landscape and I think of far off vineyards and shaded olive groves. The moon is amber coloured and magical as the swifts and swallows change shifts with the pipistrelle bats. Moths flutter like weightless wraiths as they search for the night-scented stocks and other floral perfumeries. Home, where is home? I could lie here forever in the crepuscular warmth watching the first stars as they pierce the velvet darkness of the sky. The stars, yes, they were our home; everything we're made of was cooked in the centre of the stars – transferred with light and love to blood and bone. We are in contact with the stars – physically, mentally, and spiritually. The nightjar's monotonous, melancholy song drifts towards Danbury Ridge and an owl hoots. The moon is delving the canal – a ripe cheese; an enigmatic face, a silvered sub-mariner. 'Home is where the heart is' and I'm well and truly at home by the Navigation. But bed and duty call and I must leave the night to the moon, the stars, and to the dawn mist; as white as a spectre over land fulfilled by harvest.

The author – high summer - Ulting

Beginning of Langford Cut - Beeleigh

Sea lock – Heybridge Basin

Langford Mill

Mill Beach

The Mill Beach Inn

AUGUST
POEMS:

STARS OF BETHLEHEM
(Ulting Church:: grave of a young girl burnt to death accidentally in the nineteenth century)

Shattered, is the peace of Sunday –
The river's glass turns fragments in the wake
Of every craft that cuts its thin resistance.

Somewhere a child laughs
And the sound's sharp pitch
Scratches the surface of a lucid moment.

I turn towards the church –
Walk quietly, like a ghost, across the grass,
To where a few small stars
Brink from the borders of neglected graves.

Somewhere a child laughs –
No-one hears, so no-one answers.

Doves in a low dirge
Cloud the perceptions through a trance of leaves;
And the slow light dancing
Delves to the shadows of inscripted stone.

WILLOW CUTTING

More like autumn than summer:
The men, cutting willows –
Burning branches.

Smoke lies thick across the river:
The wheat-fields, gold –
The distance, blueish.

I watch the moorhens in the shallows:
Ticking, like clockwork –
Heads nodding.

The terns are on patrol:
Hovering an instant –
Dipping to their own reflections.

Swallows will soon be gathering:
Swifts already gone –
The cuckoo also.

Spiderlings are lofted under silk:
Rise on the warming air –
Drift in dispersals.

Soon the geese in gaggles will return:
Skeins on a blue glaze –
Cracks in the pattern.

A RICH PRESERVE

All can remember blackberrying:
Each, their own lane or riverside walk –
An alley through a dark copse,
Or the field's blue edge
Shaded to corners under clumps of elm.

All have encountered the richest smells:
The sweet-dank tips of the fingers,
Prickled and purple –
Remember the leaves in red-green whorls,
Fading to yellow at the hint of autumn.

Nothing quite as succulently tells
Of summers past or winters yet to come:
The last slow heat,
The dying wasp,
The fly's deep drone –
Dreaming and drowsing through its glint
Metallics.

All have the oozings of their own nostalgia –
Their own brim jars, crammed and compacted
With the fruits of distance.

Lammas, First fruits, *Hlaf-mass* (Loaf-mass), Lughnasad. There are so many different names for the beginning of harvest. *Hlaf-mass:* the Anglo Saxon Feast of Bread when John Barleycorn is sacrificed for the good of his children. Lughnasad: the celebration of the Celtic God Lugh who gave his name to London (Lugdunum). The festival celebrated the death and resurrection of Lugh as grain God and is still celebrated by practitioners of the

'Old Religion'. First fruits: apples and pears and plums are ripening along with the taste buds and the first whiff of cider permeates the atmosphere. The flower of the month is the poppy and all along the Chelmer valley the golden corn is spattered with the blood of Persephone. Daughter of Demeter (another name for Ceres where the word cereal comes from) risen from Hades to share in the sultry and soporific heat of the harvest and the August sun. Perhaps more 'factually' the poppies should be associated with the God Cronos who after being castrated was no longer fertile and was subsequently sacrificed with a sickle – his blood, symbolised by scarlet poppies, bringing fertility to the earth. The tree of the month is the hazel. The Celts call it coll and believe that as hazel nuts fell into a particular river they were eaten by salmon and the number they ate gave them the number of spots on their bodies. They are also associated with wisdom and the salmon is said to be the wisest fish that swims. Hazel and water are almost synonymous in magic and folklore and its branches are still used for making magical wands and dowsing-rods.

I am standing by Ulting church and the sun is so intense and sections of the river so dazzling it's almost impossible to look at them. A yellowhammer is wheezing its ubiquitous summer song and the Frisian cattle are moving like slow clouds through the butter-cupped grazing meadows with their cleg-swishing tails adding to the illusion of some landlocked, hazy semaphore. All Saints; a 13th century edifice was much restored in 1873 when the north porch was added. The wooden turret and spire are a 15th century addition and the numerous holes in the shingles are the visible evidence of a particularly irreligious green woodpecker! I wander around the graveyard as I have done so many times before. I am forever drawn to the grave of Eliza Gozzet a child accidentally burnt to death in the 19th century. Stars of Bethlehem are blooming around her grave – somehow appropriately it seems to me. Simple white stars with thin green sepals on their undersides – symbols of purity and love. When I see the snowdrops in the winter or the Calvary clover in summer I always think of little Eliza – poor little Eliza. So many births, marriages and deaths recorded in the earth and stone of this beautifully spiritual place: how many people through the centuries have arrived at the south door by barge to celebrate mass, a baptism, a marriage or to mourn their departed loved-ones? In the cottage gardens the buddleia is in full bloom. Commas, small and large tortoiseshells, cabbage whites, peacocks, red admirals and painted ladies, sip at the honeyed nectars and flutter around like bright spirits from the past. Speckled woods flicker in and out of the tree-lined arbours, sun-shot and golden shafted in their timeless, immemorial flight. This is high summer and the doves know it: the ' voice of the turtle' is a sleepy, romantic song, evocative of August, accompanied by ring and collared doves as they deliver their muted decibels from the vantage of tall and dusky summer trees. The stock dove tries to join in but only manages a gruff, coughing double note that somehow spoils the syllabic drowsiness of its more somnolent and summery kith and kin. I look out across the fields towards Rushes lock. The lake is as glint as platinum in the sunlight and a number of anglers shelter under their green umbrellas as they wait for the carp to rise to their floating baits. Terns patrol the river – as white and incongruous as snow – then hover for an eternal instant before they drop like fathoming iconoclasts to shatter their own holy and reflective images. The mysterious figwort blooms and its flowers are like clots of congealed blood along the burnished edges of the igneous river bank. It is time for a siesta; it's too hot to fish, too hot to sleep in either the sunlight or the shade and far too hot for everything except the drone and stridulation of innumerable insects. I must leave this pastoral paradise that's been ignited by the fires of an infernal August and make my perspiring way back to my homestead and its cool and shaded corners.

The harvest is in full swing. Combine harvesters and tractors and trailers are quartering the fields like mechanical short-eared owls. Dust is drifting everywhere on the breeze; a thick and acrid musty smoke that pinches the nostrils and irritates the eyes. Rabbits and rats are in a panic as they move towards the centre of the fields to avoid the combines. The farmers have been lucky this year, the summer storms have held off so far and it looks as though the harvest will be gathered in without any problems. Thistledown is blowing across the fields and along the river, as incongruous as the diving terns, an illusory winter's blizzard in the season of the blazing sun. Spiderlings are lofted on their own shimmering silks to be carried on the thermals to unknown and unwary distant destinations. The rosebay willow-herb's profusion of summer flowers are turning to a delicate, silvery floss by the roadside verges and thoughts of portending mist form in the feathery shadows of its presence. Its other name is 'fireweed' due to the fact that it is a coloniser of burnt ground. After the Blitz in London rosebay willow-herd invaded every corner of the city, like the purple ghost of nature's latent power. Another plant well known in the Chelmer valley is the Oxford ragwort: *senecio squalidus;* which I believe means squalid old man. Like the rosebay it spread rapidly from towns and cities along the railway lines and because of its Latin name I like to think of it as a hobo forever jumping trains and setting up its temporary home wherever it pleases! Field scabious is blooming everywhere, blue or lilac, pink or lavender, it's hard to say; but pale and beautiful beyond belief. Its marshland cousin, the Devil's bit scabious, gets its name because its roots (like all members of the scabious family) are extremely short. It's said that because the root of the plant was so good for curing ailments the devil bit it off short so as to negate its beneficial properties! The augers are working overtime, the granaries are full and the drying lofts loud with the sound of hot, expelling air. Loaves are being baked from the first sheaves and corn dollies woven by superstitious hands. A night the stubble fields are pale and ghostly under the harvest moon as if a frost had touched the dews of dying August. It is the season for gleaning. Gleaning as much of nature's bounty as a generous Mother Earth will allow her mortal and ever-thankful worshippers. Dawn takes on the hint of approaching autumn. Everything is spidery and damp. Geometries of silk spangle in the sun-shot, misted hedgerows and blackberries cluster like succulent bruises from the flesh of the multicoloured briar. I walk along the towpath towards Rushes lock and pick and eat the delicious musky fruits growing beside the navigation. The sun is getting hot again and the mist is dispersing. The swallows and martins are gathering in loose flocks and the swifts have already made their journey southwards. The insects' chorus starts up again, wasps and metallic flies coruscate in the brambles, and crickets and grasshoppers rasp away at the increasing August heat. By noon the first cumulous clouds have started to appear in the sky. It is hot and humid, just the perfect conditions for a summer storm. By early afternoon the cumuli have billowed enormously over the Danbury Ridge. The tops are glacial and white but the bases of the clouds are blackening ominously. One of the banks of cloud is forming a thunderhead and the first stroke of forked lightning is followed by a dull reverberation. The sky is closing in completely as patches of sapphire blue are erased by the bruising darkness. All is still; unbelievably still and silent. The first large drops of summer rain spatter amongst the flickering leaves on the alders and interlocking concentric circles give the river's surface the appearance of cogs and wheels – like some clockwork mechanism! Three separate forks of lightning strike Danbury Ridge simultaneously and the sky cracks and cackles as the rain comes on in earnest. The rain is torrential and all distances disappear in the veils of precipitation. Thunder and lightning is near continuous and hailstones the size of pigeons eggs clatter on the brickwork and the lock-gates. I'm drenched and somewhat nervous at being out in a thunderstorm as violent as this. In the Chelmer's flat, valley-bottom landscape, it would be too dangerous to shelter beneath the trees as a direct strike would be eminently possible. As I make my way back towards the car the river is rising fast and a number of nests – belonging to different species of waterfowl – race past me in the swirling torrential waters. Not a moment too soon the rain begins to ease and a rift in the clouds allows a shaft of returning sunlight to illuminate the uncanny summer darkness. A rainbow forms in the east against the blackness of the receding storm and shimmering silver droplets of rain glitter like falling coins. The sun intensifies and everything starts to steam in the earth scented atmosphere. The rainbow doubles: rainbows and sunlight, black clouds and blue sky, steam and silver droplets in the trees – paradise regained; summer reasserted. I am a part of the weather and the weather is a part of me. Water responds to water, flesh to the weather's spirit, mind to the skylarks and the gilded cumuli. Poppies and scabious, mayweed and cranesbill, encompass me with colour as I drive through the country lanes and a pheasant, like a kaleidoscopic thought, crosses the windscreen as it continues on its immortal journey through the sweet and scented summerlands of infinite love and timeless eternal light.

August is coming to an end and I make my way to the back-stream at Hoe Mill for some late summer chub fishing. I have fished this particular stream since I was a boy; I'm now nearing sixty years of age and I'm still as excited by the prospect of a 5lb chub as I ever was. Chub; treasure buried deep in the roots of alders – frog gulpers, cheese swallowers, harbingers of rashes through the swathes of nettles, producers of fevers in the name of gold. I look into the water's crystal ball and scry for fish. I toss in a few pieces of bread-flake and wait for a response. It isn't long in coming. Three or four enormous chub sidle out into the stream and suck in my anticipatory offerings. I'm tackled up with a sturdy, 10 foot carbon fibre rod, a fixed spool reel, 6lb line and a number 8 hook. I bait up with a flake of bread the size of a 50 pence piece and freeline it upstream of the overhanging alders.

One of the monsters rises to the bait; sucks it in, swirls and dives for the bottom. I strike and the battle is on. The rod bends violently and the clutch on the reel starts to give. But I can't give it any line; I must stop it in its tracks before it gains the snag-ridden safety of the alder roots. It makes a series of powerful plunges before I eventually manage to turn its head – it's nearly beaten and I manage to draw it out from under the bank and into deeper water. It comes to the waiting net crashing through the crystal spray of its own energetic making. It gradually tires, lays flat on the surface, and I draw it over the net. The prize is mine; the prospector assays the river's ore, and the fever abates: 5lbs of incomparable gold with a mouth as round and astounded as Munch's 'The Scream' – perfection personified; a dream, manifested in daylight. August is coming to an end. The light is lower and less intense – shadows are longer. There is a stillness that whispers of September. The robin's autumnal song lilts like a lamentation from the leaf-altering trees both by day and by night. Tree creepers scurry and search for food on the trunks of ash and oak. Blackcaps skulk in the undergrowth and the reed warblers unwind their summer ratchets as the call of the south stills them to silence and the twitch of wings. The first bonfires coil their smoke from the cottage gardens and windfalls lie and ferment in the cidery orchards. Finches in many-coloured, foraging flocks, flit and twitter across the stubbled fields and rooks and jackdaws carry the starlit dusk on their black, prophetic pinions. September is upon us. The first fallen leaves drift across the weir at Paper Mills by North Hill at Little Baddow; Canada geese clank down the cooling airways to roost on the lakes by Hoe mill, and the burdock sets its spiked and clinging seeds – pregnant with purpose and another summer. Thistles gather their charms of goldfinches and teasels turn to sandy brown and amethyst. I remove my hook from the line, wind the line onto the reel, and dismantle my rod. A crescent moon hangs in the evening sky like the pairing of a giant's fingernail and the first, faint stars twinkle with iridescence. An owl hoots, a fox barks, and a heron crashes ungainly into its leafy roost. Farewell summer, farewell the cuckoo and the swift; the caterpillar and the moth. The Perseids have finished with their silvery showers and Boreas waits beyond the Land of the Midnight Sun with his cold and ghosted breath. The river swallows the stars and the crescent moon, and light becomes a memory – a once and faded dream. Farewell to my timeless summer; to the dog rose and the loosestrife and the ever-golden chalice of the lily – farewell my friends; farewell.

Beeleigh lock looking towards the Spinney

Below Boreham – Sandon Brook is on the right

Hoe Mill lock

Ulting church – late summer

Grace's cottages – near Grace's Walk

The ford - Riffhams

SEPTEMBER
POEMS:

SEPTEMBER MORNING

This morning is north-easterly and
Cirrus – where blue astride the meaning of
The sky divides in two with one long strand

Of vapour. The aircraft moves through silence
On its journey – from where to where I do
Not need to know – as journeys – in a sense –

Are what we are. Perhaps we had to choose –
But now forget the purpose and the plan
In that one reason – that rounds the plum and bruises

All the sloes. Listen to the robin: that's enough –
Is all you need of temperament and tense
To know the muted odyssey of love.

There is in this chill morning – drenched with dew –
A destination – you – can understand.

SWALLOW MUSIC

A strange notation on the wires –
Crotchet and quaver
To the sky's grey music.

Larghetto, in a symphony of leaves,
As down the scale
They deepen into gold.

Accompaniment to windfalls in the mist,
Where light is strung
Through air – violoncello.

WORDS FOR AUTUMN

Autumn poems are the best –
Poems when the year is at the turn
And words are blessed, like leaves across the wind.

Time for the bramble and the wasp –
When morning fields are spidery and wet
And breath is lost, like ghosts upon the air.

A place where the fruits are ripe –
Where the blackthorn holds each berry with a bloom
That chooses light dissolving into mist.

A sky – September blue –
Where geese that fly in loose unwritten lines
Decry the news of winter in their wake.

'Season of mists and mellow fruitfulness', young Keats had it right, he knew the feel of the time exactly. The orchard trees are buckling under the fructifying weight of their precious bounty. Victoria plums, as red and rich as rubies, glisten in the sun-striated mist. Golden pears hang like glimmering lanterns in the shadows and the burnishing crop of delicious apples are as ripe and ruddy-faced as tenant farmers. Bulging greengages tempt my lips with the sweet-remembered taste of passing youth, and the bullace vies with codlings and James Grieves to touch the plangent note of all nostalgia. There are windfalls everywhere – a cache of nature's treasure nestling in the orchard grasses amongst the daisies and the dandelions. The sweet-sharp smell of fermentation pervades the misted atmosphere and drunken wasps and starlings swig and stagger in the sun's inebriation. Endless flocks of ravenous finches are gleaning the stubble in the pale and distant fields and the wires cling to swallows – strung like pearls. In the shadowy hedge bottoms, the cuckoo pint – 'lords and ladies', 'parson in the pulpit', or 'Adam and Eve' – lifts its towers of red-resplendent, yet deadly poisonous berries, into the fathoming shafts of early autumn sunlight. A robin sings, the swallows twitter and the small gnats dance and mourn. Fungi of all descriptions appear as if from nowhere to tease us with their equinoctial mysteries. Blewitt and blusher, stinkhorn and cep, death-cap and destroying angel, lift their uncanny, spore-emboldened heads and dare us to sample their dank and dark fecundity. Fairy ring champignons cover the meadows with shadowy, supernatural circles and our minds and collective memories dance through the dreams of Puck and pure Titania. The fly agarics, red with white spots and looking as though they've been plastic moulded by machines – skulk in the undergrowth by the silver birches and deal in hallucinogenic drugs. A Viking clan, the Berserkers, used to chew small pieces of them before they went into battle – and they literally went 'berserk'! I make my way along the back roads from Hoe Mill to Beeleigh. I park at the bottom of the lane beyond the abbey and then walk to the lock gates and the weir. This is where the Rivers Chelmer and Blackwater meet before crossing the weir and mingling with Maldon's tidal waters. The tide is at half ebb and there is water everywhere. Shattered and decaying elms point their gnarled and crooked fingers to the sky, and a pair of swans drift like a dream of the arctic through the whispering reeds. Maldon's small eminence rises from the purpling mist and crowns September with a jumble of ancient buildings. A curlew flutes its lost and lonely song and time and tide defy their passing adage and stand as still and as permanent as rock. I watch as the only waterfall in Essex is held – as in aspic – in my mind's eternal eye as coots and moorhens petrify before me in the depth of the moment's brooding and infinite stillness. A mullet levitates above the river for an instant and then crashes back into a silvered concentricity as time and timelessness

117

coincide. A horse-drawn barge, loaded with timber cut from the Ygdrasill – the enchanted ash, sacred to Woden, whose roots and trunk and branches range throughout the entire universe – makes its way beside the Long Pond and the harness bells and brasses jangle in the distance like St Peter's gold and oft-times fabled keys. The barge Victoria passes through the lock and makes way to its moorings at Heybridge Basin and its wake is as white as the water cascading over the weir. The gentle thrum of its engine is accompanied by the cry of black-headed gulls as they curve across the blue-unbounded realms of a soft September sky. Who could not be a poet in a world as pure and pristine as today's? A ghostly sailing vessel drifts along Langford Cut towards the sea and Norsey, Osea and Mersea Islands float on the blear-autumnal tides of their past and future histories.

September is the time for roach. Roach and elderberries are as good as synonymous – partners in perfection. Between the Sugar Mill cottages and Ricketts lock there is a spot where brambles and elders hang out across the river and the roach form large shoals to feed on the fathoming fruits of summer's maturing succulence. Elderberry wine and blackberry preserve – not just the preserve of mankind, but food for the chaffinch and the prince of fishes. I set up my roach-pole and groundbait with some grains of hempseed. The first fallen leaves form a mosaic on the river's velvet surface. I take an elderberry from the tree, pierce it with a 16 hook, and ship it out into the gentle flow. The float dips and disappears and I'm into my first prime roach. Fish are coming to the net at regular intervals – beautiful pink-bellied, river-smelling, goer roach. Unless you're a fisherman, and especially a roach fisherman, you may not understand the ecstasy and privilege I'm talking about! To be connected to two worlds by rod and line, to live in the conscious temporal realms but at the same time to fathom the watery depths of the limitless unconscious. To hold in one's human hands the silver-scaled and ruby-encrusted denizens of distant stars and deep, untroubled

118

waters, is a privilege indeed – an ecstatic, heavenly privilege. Fishermen love fish; like 'primitive' peoples they honour them – worship them even. The roach is my totem animal – my link to the world of spirit and beyond. The elder tree is said to be unlucky – Christ was supposedly crucified upon an elder and Judas, it is said, hung himself from one! But it is also a protective tree; one planted near the house should protect you from witches, and twigs laid over a grave will guard the interred body from the interference of evil spirits – or so legend and folklore suggest! The wine, whether made from its spring flowers – clear, cool, sparkling and refreshing – or its autumn berries – red, rich, fruitful and full-bodied – is simply delicious. I've often eaten the berries straight from the tree and why such sweet and succulent fruits are not more utilized in the culinary arts, eludes me. It is nearly dusk and the harvest moon is almost golden as it rises resplendent from the eastern horizon. The triple Goddess – dependant on its phases it is either the maiden the mother or the crone. Cast your spells for increase as it waxes and for decrease as it wanes – cast them in honour of the Huntress, the Lady of the night eternal; the Goddess of fertility. Fish are rising everywhere. Roach, rudd and dace, offer their sacred silver to the distant stars; and the stars respond by coming down to delve the holy waters of the river. The day is dying and the Pleiades are reborn. Light and dark, night and day, death and resurrection – wheels with wheels, the cycles of the year, the cycles of our lives and their correspondences – the snake consumes its own tail; no-one is born, so no-one dies – all is one, all is endless. I make my way back along the river to Sugar Mill cottages. The air is growing chill and a thin white mist is forming on the surface of the navigation. Fires are lift in the hearths and smoke – like genies released from bottles – rises to touch the twilight and the stars. Lights from the cottage windows are reflected in the canal's abysmal depths and a hare scuttles along the towpath, like a splash of liquid silver. What begins must end and what ends must be renewed. I walk through the copse to my waiting car

119

and leaves, like angel's wings, fathom the moonlight in a whispering drift of glint and golden silence.

The month moves on and the equinox is heralded by gales. Swallows, house martins and sand martins, drift southwards in increasing numbers, the curlews have started to return from their moorland breeding grounds and the occasional fieldfares plunder the hawthorns on their Viking wings. Flocks of lapwings are an ever-shifting checker board of coruscating plumage as they traverse the blue dimensions of the sky. The sun is beginning to lose its power and life is slowing down in readiness for winter. The apple tree is appropriate to the equinoctial season: the Hesperides – the gardens or the Isles of the Blest – where the three mythical sisters guarded the golden apples. The Isle of Avalon where King Arthur was taken after his final battle is not just a term for the Celtic 'otherworld' but also means the isle of apples. The Lady of the Wildwoods, Diana, Goddess of the sacred groves, is associated with the symbols of the apple tree and the deer and the Celtic Goddess Nemhain is often depicted with an apple branch in her hand. The unicorn also rested beneath an apple tree representing immortality through wisdom and could only be tamed by a virgin. Blackberry and apple pie, roasted apples and cinnamon, cider and apple juice – wisdom indeed! Below Boreham, Sandon Brook enters the River Chelmer from the south and I stand by the confluence and watch as workers from the Navigation Company fell some of the willows beside the river. These are 'cricket bat willows' renowned worldwide for the quality of their timber. They're felled about every 15 years and replaced with a 'set' or willow pole so as to continue the profitable rotation. The men are burning the leaves and the unwanted branches and smoke, like a blue ghost, drifts across the river and the fields on its blear and spectral journey. Wood-smoke is the epitome of autumn; its sweet-cum-acrid fragrance somehow redolent of death and corruption. 'Now is the time for the burning of the leaves', Laurence Binyon's poem about reflection, loss, and ultimate renewal, says it all really. I go back to the car and drive off towards Sandon Bridge on the A 414 just west of Danbury. I've stood on this bridge so many times in the past and still hope to do so many times in the future. The brook runs over a sill and in the relatively slack water beyond it a shoal of small, wild brown trout, undulate with their heads against the flow. The bushes are thick with berries: rose hips and sloes, haws and the occasional snowberry. Will it be a hard winter; or was it just a good summer – who knows, the meteorologist or the countryman? The trout are spotted with iridescence: oil on water, starlight in frost, sinuous rainbows. I've caught them before – the proper way, with a dry fly! I'm not really a fly fisherman but I've had my fair share of rudd and dace on flies as well as the occasional brown trout. But today I'm not fishing – just observing. Apart from the sound of the traffic I'm at perfect peace with the world. My mind undulates with the trout, is finned and stippled with rainbows; is attuned to water. Danbury's ancient church rises some 360 feet above me to the east and Chelmsford's modern commercial and industrial conurbation lies silent in the chill, polluted, sun-declining distance of the west. Here there is peace and calm and clear air – natural transcendence. I am a long way from the navigation but its spirit travels up the currents of this brook in the shape of a solitary chub. I can tell it by the thickness of its head, its wide and ravenous mouth as it ripples like a mirage under water. Fish, fish, fish; what is it with me and fish? Why the seeming affinity? Water of course – water and life; emotional water that falls as tears, the breaking waters of birth, water that baptises or consecrates the coffins of the dead. It's said that the planet earth is made up of five sevenths water and holds the same volume of the precious liquid as it always has – it's just recycled! It can be solid, liquid or gaseous. Are we made of light or water – spirit or substance or both? Ice, fluid, steam; transformations, epiphanies, mysteries – all life is water, as frost it even breaks the obstinacy of stone – invigorates the living soil. Do fish drink, will a sinking man drown – all is a mystery my friends; an infinite mystery. The last of the September sun catches the surface of the brook and I understand something of 'the dazzling darkness'; 'the thoughtless all-knowing'. Venus – the Goddess of love – sheds her evening light across the valley and at Riffhams a moon-silvered pike; half in and half out of the water, slithers its muscular way across the shallows of the ford. Blake's Wood is wreathed in enveloping darkness save where a moon-enlightened splash of liquid mercury spatters the tree-trunks and the dew-benighted carpet of the leaves. Are the stars made of water – are they dead or alive? They are not water but they produce everything that's needed for its precipitation – they are God's chemists; Love's laboratory. I drive across the bridge below Boreham and the river's silver artery carries its platelets of moonlight and starlight from the fertile, chalk-encrusted hills of northern Essex all the way to Heybridge and the salt-eternal whisper of the seas. Water is life; life is water – the clouds build, the river meanders, the ice forms, the steam rises after summer rain. Soft September, dewed and misted, is coming to an end and a flood of moisture trickles down my chin as I bite deeply into a large and golden pear. Water my friends – water. Honour the fish; they are your brothers and sisters under the skin; fellow travellers from the stars – spirit and substance both; denizens of a dream – as miraculous as bread, kindred of starlight and the Virgin's sacred womb.

Michaelmas and September finally dies. Did St George really kill the dragon or did the legend come from the much older story of Michael, Prince of Light, who tamed the Dragon of Knowledge? How many churches on the tops of hills are dedicated to St Michael? They must be nearly numberless. The Bible says that Michael held power over the heavens, like the earlier Eros who created the firmament. Michael is no dragon killer, he comes to terms with the beast, harnesses the random, primeval energy of fire - brings order out of chaos. Michaelmas daisies are blooming everywhere. Pale, not quite pink and not quite purple, they merge almost perfectly with the sun-shot, misted remnants of this mellow and ever-fruitful month. Most of the swallows and martins have gone south as just a few lone stragglers flit and twitter backwards and forwards from the looping wires of the telegraph poles. 'Time is away and somewhere else' wrote Louis MacNeice in one of his most famous poems and summertime is certainly far away on the wings of migrating birds. A bloom of sea asters softens the greens and greys of the creeks and saltings between Beeleigh and Maldon as a pair of flying shelduck laugh their eerie laugh across the tideways and the marshes. Along the lane by the abbey the brambles still offer up a profusion of succulent berries, but country folk say that it's unlucky to pick blackberries after Michaelmas Day as on that day the Devil fell from heaven and cursed and spat on the bush after landing in and amongst its thorns - pick them if you dare! The navigation makes its journey – as does the year. From Springfield Basin to the sea; past mills or the sites of long departed mills, under 200 year old original bridges, through locks and over cascading weirs and even that rarity of all rarities in Essex - a waterfall. This was the end of the Celtic year – the pastoral year. Beasts were slaughtered and pickled, smoked and salted for the winter table. The harvest had been gathered in and fruit, cereals and root vegetables were dried and put in store. What with supermarkets and freezers, factory farming and world trade, we seem to have lost our affinity with the seasons of the agricultural year and yet here along the secluded country byways of the Chelmer valley the past reasserts itself. Orchard and cottage garden, farmland and village allotment are all busy with the final days of harvest. Country churches display the fruits of the land with thankfulness to God and the grateful parishioners sing the traditional rural hymns. Folk singers re-enact the bucolic past with songs of the turning seasons and sing their landlocked, sea-salty shanties from the comfort of dry and antiquated inns - and why not indeed? I for one enjoy the vicarious nostalgia – all the pleasure without the pain, no less! Michaelmas is almost over – September teeters on the shivering edge of cold October and the mist across the river at Beeleigh thickens into fog. The trees drip silver droplets and a robin's lonesome threnody can offer but a melancholy joy. A siren sounds in the east and the bells on distant buoys reverberate in my sea-salted imagination. Sails are furled in Collier's Reach and bargees ferry their unloaded cargoes through the grey, uncharted waters of a dank and dismal early Victorian afternoon. I, the living, remember the dead: the men who worked the schooners and the brigs, the Thames barges and the canal lighters. I remember the draught horses, the lock keepers, their wives and families, the merchants and the farm labourers, the navvies and the engineers – I remember them all, every last one of them. September dies to the sounds of chains and winches out at sea and my mind's irrepressible magic conjures the seamen of another age – dancing their hornpipes and downing - in one -their swigs of imported rum.

Harvest reflections - Ulting

The barge 'Victoria' – Heybridge Basin

Original bridge – near Sandford lock

Paper Mills lock

The Old Ship – Heybridge Basin

The Jolly Sailor – Heybridge Basin

St Bartholomew's - Wickham Bishops

OCTOBER
POEMS:
AUTUMN MANUSCRIPT

At All Saints beside the Chelmer
There's a reverential glare
That illuminates the seasonal demise;
Where transitional recorders
Are as legible as prayer
And the trees wear autumn vestments as a guise.

On the river's swirling parchment
A calligraphy of leaves
Has been gilded by the impress of the sun;
In the sky a faint disorder
Is a scrawling line of geese
Who have flighted as the ink begins to run.

In the context of the weather
There are paragraphs of light
That dispel the solemn litany of rain;
Incunabula, together
With the manuscripts of sight
Show the primal urge to worship and explain.

Out across the water meadows
As all histories condense
There's the chilling obfuscation of the mist;
Where the quill outlives the feather
In the ordering of tense
And the runes of partiality persist.

Like a medieval rubric
Or the imprint of a seal
The distended sun steals silently away;
Is the landscape as it's written
One apocryphal or real –
Are the furrows still indicative of clay?

CANADA GEESE

The Canadas are feeding on the wheat –
When evening comes they'll rise above the fields
And beat the bounds of autumn with their wings.

They'll draw their threads of sound across the sky,
Like signatures, half-written by the wind
That sighs through trees and scatters tears of gold.

On frosted air they'll slide towards their roost –
Like angels, down an elemental stair,
To prove themselves the deities of ice.

HUNTER'S MOON

This is a night
For the river.

Not a word's breath
Quivers its question
Through unanswered leaves.

The silence
Listens to itself –
Sinks to the echo
Of inverted vision.

A mist
Transliterates
From air –
Layers its language
With a level tongue.

Somehow
The stars
Resist –
Shift their assumptions
Into iridescence.

The moon reflects
A virtue of its own –
Mouths the phonetic
Into double zero.

October is the tenth month of the year and yet its name derives from the Latin *octo* whereby it was the eighth month of the year in the Roman calendar. Now the leaves are really beginning to turn and the countryside is awash with greens and golds, reds and yellows, and the Virginia creeper covering the brickwork of some of the surrounding houses takes on an almost fluorescent scarlet colouring. The first frosts of the year are encouraging the leaves to fall more rapidly and the river's surface is kaleidoscopic with drifting foliage. The blazing horse chestnut candles of May have turned into the spiky fruits of conkers and the squirrels are moving like silver waves under the golden boughs of the sweet chestnut trees. Hazelnuts hang from their 'fairy caps' and raucous jays are ferrying acorns to their winter stores in all the valley woodlands. The Anglo Saxons called the month both *wynmonath* (wine month) and *winterfyllith* (referring to October's full moon which denoted the beginning of winter). Whatever, nature's storehouse is certainly bountiful and provisions are being harvested by all and sundry in preparation for the colder months to come. Ploughing has started in earnest and lone tractors are trawling their shoals of seagulls across the fields adjoining the water meadows. The weather this month can be as changeable as in March: dead calm and foggy, cold and frosty, wet and windy, or as warm as August with an Indian summer.

At this time of year I always take a walk along Bumfords Lane near Ulting. Despite the ravages of Dutch elm disease there are still plenty of elms along the lane whose bark is not fissured wide enough to allow entry to the elm beetles and their offending fungus. Apart from the field maple elm leaves are the most yellowy leaves I know. It is almost surreal to walk along Bumfords Lane in October. The colour is supernatural and it's so dazzling it's like walking inside a light-bulb. The lane is crisp and carpeted with its precious cargo and the congealed clots of late blackberries add an uncanny contrast to the furnace of light and lyrical, lonesome robins. Fieldfares chack as they fly overhead in pillaging flocks and the first redwings compete with the resplendent robins for redness as they return from the tundra and the distant Arctic wastes. Canada Geese drag their clanking chains across the solitary blue confinement of a blear October sky and magpies chatter in their brash and bullying flocks. I am encased in gold, entombed in an aureate sepulchre, jailed in a jaundiced heaven. In my imagination's hand I hold the keys of St Peter and although it's autumn the 'summerlands' are mine for the taking. Leaves are falling like glint and golden feathers shaken from the wings of angels. Cherubim and seraphim fly in the form of starlings and lapwings overhead and as I come out of the lane and into the fields leading up to Rushes lock candles of yellowing toadflax flare from the pallid verges like a votive fire. Rooks caw, jackdaws chack, and the whispering sound of unnumbered wings spills from the flocks of starlings as they spiral and twist and turn like erratic wisps of inviolable smoke. Toadflax: *linaria vulgaris, linaria* meaning linear, like the leaves of the true flax and *vulgaris* meaning common. But why does it have the prefix 'toad'? It was once given the name *bubonium* which could have been mistaken for the Latin *bufonium* which is derived from *bufo* – meaning toad! Or it could just simply mean 'false flax' or a plant that the toad likes to shelter beneath – who knows? The River Ter trickles under the lane and its ever-rippling waters capture the sunlight and the sky's cerulean vault. Pied wagtails flicker like strobe lighting as they fly along the riverbank and a kingfisher lights its own metallic fuse as its bursts, spontaneously, into blue and orange flames. Danbury Ridge is vaguely purpled and misted and I seem to transcend the moment as the sun assays its golden handiwork. From Barnes Mill to Beeleigh lock and falls October is reflected in the sunlit, gilded waters of the glorious Navigation where gulls curve and cry on salt-white wings and carrion crows double their darkness in St Luke's unfathomable mirror. Summer it seems is endless; sans swallows, sans swifts, sans cuckoos, or anything else the pedant would say authenticates the dates on the calendar. I praise all the Gods and Goddesses of all of mankind's magnificent and multifarious religions for giving me life and love on such a day as this as the sun sinks slowly from its zenith and journeys down the blue-unbounded sky to keep its blushing assignation with twilight and the silver lips of a sensual venus.

The old-man's-beard is fully blown and venerable in the surrounding hedgerows and the ivy's autumn flowering gathers its wasps and the ever-startling red-admirals. I'm going roach fishing on the concrete apron under the overarching water main near Sugar Mill Cottages. I pass the deep hole by the wooden footbridge where I've caught so many stupendous summer perch. There is hardly any flow on the river and I feel as though I could walk across the multicoloured carpet of the leaves. It is calm and misted and sunlit, and the occasional fish stipples the surface with concentric gold. Starlings murmur in the oaks and ring-doves remember summer with their songs. A heron flies like an airborne ghost across the river, lifts its wings, back peddles, and then stands on its stilted legs in the shallows with all the military aplomb and erectness of a sentry on guard duty. The cottages look so sure of themselves and somehow unassailable in the dazzling doldrums of this late October day and yet this is the very month when a few days of heavy rain could see them flooded and surrounded by the unpredictable waters of this most changeable of seasons. There is still some mallow flowering along the towpath and the ever-ubiquitous dandelions scatter their gold doubloons in all directions. I set up stall on the concrete apron and tackle up. I loose feed with some gentles and hemp and start to trot the swim. Just to the east of me is a stretch of the river known as 'bream bend' where I once saw the results of electro-fishing and was astounded by the amount and quality of the fish coming from a place that I've fished all my life. There were bream to 8lbs, roach and rudd well over 2lbs, perch to 3lbs, tench to 5lbs, numerous river carp and a pike that must have been nearer 30lbs than 20! My float dips just a fraction of an inch and I strike – I'm into my first roach. I can't go wrong; whether I used gentles or hemp it doesn't seem to matter. Fish after fish is coming to the net, and good fish too, all goer roach between about a ½ and ¾'s of a pound. I fish for a couple of hours in the clemency of St Luke's most hallowed summer and then a flock of lapwing darken the en-clouding sapphire of the sky with portents of imminent rain and so I decide to call it a day. As I walk back along the towpath to the car the rain begins to fall. The mosaic of the leaves upon the river is interspersed by the concentricity of raindrops. Are they raindrops or are they rising fish? They are both of course – manifestations of life; universal spirals radiating from the heart of God. The sun drifts in and out of the gathering nimbus and striations of diagonal light connect the earth to the realms of the higher self – the infinitely vast and everlasting, celestial spirit. A robin sings its sweet and muted song and the music of the spheres expands with its own aerial concentricity. I can hear the soft rain pattering on the crispness the fallen leaves and that indescribable dank and delicious scent of autumn permeates the misted and moistened atmosphere. A mink swims sinuously across the river and its sleek, black form highlights the reds and yellows of the floating leaves. Ring-doves remember summer with their drowsy songs as they hunch up their feathers against the increasing rain. The wind starts to blow in erratic gusts and a fathoming trail of detaching leaves sidles in a golden swathe towards the decomposing mulch of a deep and delirious harlequinade – enacted sublimely, on the bright October waters.

Samhaine or Halloween, call it what you will, Christian or Pagan it doesn't matter. The veil is thin and we are closer to our ancestors than at any other time of the year. Stand by the lock gates at Hoe Mill – can't you smell the coal, the flour; the horses? Can't you hear the steady toll of hooves as the barges make their lumbering way towards Chelmsford? Can you not hear the lock keeper's children singing and skipping or see the freshly laundered clothes blowing on the washing-line? Samhaine, the end of the pagan year and also its beginning: the cycles turn – Alpha to Omega; omega back to Alpha. Now is the time to try and catch the last falling leaves; more difficult than it seems – they evade the grasp; fly off in all directions. It is the West Wind Sabbat – the western quarter of the elemental circle. At Samhaine the moon is known as the Elder Tree Moon; the personification of the crone – the third face of the Goddess. You should always ask the 'old girl' politely when you want to pick her flowers in spring or her berries in autumn – or else!!! Herbs linked to this time of year are thyme, for departed souls, and rosemary, for remembrance. Belladonna (beautiful woman?) otherwise known as deadly nightshade is the witches herb and the dried flowers and leaves can be used as an ingredient in incense to open up the psyche for astral travel. Deadly nightshade was also an ingredient of 'flying ointment' which witches applied to their bodies to give them the sensation of flying. And then there's the narrow leaved rue with its blueish leaves and yellow flowers and smelling as dank and musty as an old church – another plant associated with this season; the flower of repentance. Would you like to make Elder Rob to soothe a cold or a sore throat in the winter? Sweat some elderberries overnight on a low heat, then mix the juices with honey and warn till everything has liquefied. Add rum to taste and the remedy is ready for use – simple! I'm standing by Paper Mills lock. The trees are leafless and skeletal, the sky is overcast and the hills to the south and north are misted and losing definition. What for me is the last month of autumn (November) is nearly upon us. Save for the ever-faithful and solemn sounding robin the birds are silent; the air is chill and there's hardly a breath of wind. The river and the sky are both painted in monochrome and it's difficult to tell what are reflections and what is 'reality'. I get a pot of tea from the Old Stables Tearoom and sit at a table beside the lock. Silence is a blessing – a beatitude. I can hear the soundless heart of the universe – the voiceless voice of God. It is there in the sapless trees; in the mellow and muted canal and in the lone swan's deadened and dying aria. Look with me deep into the waters of The Chelmer & Blackwater Navigation. Can you see the ghost of November looking back at you – the sunless apparition of yourself framed in the gaunt and skeletal trees? A peewit cries and the sound's sharp and incongruous note etches the river like diamond on glass. The tea in my cup is steaming and so is my breath – two spectres; two autumnal months looking into each other's insubstantial countenances. Is it life or death – death or life? Is there a beginning and an end or is it timeless and absolute like the river's infinite gaze into the misted and equally infinite mirror of the sky – who knows? I can hear a church bell: is it coming from Danbury, Woodham Walter, Little Baddow or Ulting? Is it ringing now or in the past – or even in the future? I take my empty cup and teapot back into the tearooms and then make my way to the car park by the weir-pool. All is silent; a deep and deathly silence. I sit in my car, fill my pipe, light it and open the window. Smoke rises like a blue ghost into the still and sombre October afternoon as I turn the key in the ignition. The sudden onset of mechanical sound shatters my reverie and the canal's immovable iconography. Time reasserts itself as the engine revs, the wheels turn, and sequentiality is re-established. Along the side of North Hill the toadflax burns its votive candles and the old-man's-beard is as venerable as ever. All is in essence a valediction - a gloomy farewell to St Luke and St Michael; to summer and its harvest, September and its ripe fruits, October and its ivy-flowered butterflies drifting and drowsing towards hibernation in the gently levelling rays of a weakening and ineffectual sunlight. November must follow Samhaine with its Christian accretions of All Saints and All Souls and we must prepare ourselves for winter and the return of the crystalline and frost-attired deities who inhabit the cold and ice-remembered regions far, far, to the north of the most northerly of all embittered winds.

Another view of the 'Long Pond'

Fullbridge - Maldon

Market Hill - Maldon

Early snow - Ulting

River Ter – below Nounsley

Wickham Place – Wickham Bishops

Another view of Hatfield Peverel

TOGETHER

Let us together
Through the dying season
Walk to the corner
Of a time remembered;

Turn from the treason
Of the sighing wind,

As the last few leaves
Fall from the embers
Of forgotten fire.

Let us through ashes
Like the risen phoenix
Flare with the passion
Of a love rekindled;

Burn in the furnace
Of a far emotion,

As the first cold tear
Falls from the lesion
Of the light departed.

ROBIN

I cannot see the singer
But the song
Holds autumn in the sadness of its scale,
Like leaves that fall to realise their shadows
When gold no linger lingers nor prevails.

The sun's as pale as pebbles
Or a primrose
That finds itself a refugee from spring,
I cannot see the solitary singer
But every note has winter on its wing.

I cannot hold the summer
But its ghost
Lies golden with the lichen on the wall,
The song's as thin as something nearly over
And down the air the music floats and falls.

BLOW-OUT

A funny bloke is autumn –
A rare old windbag,
All smoke and bluster.

A brown-ale swill of a man
Frowning to furrows
In the dregs of sunlight.

He's had his fill of goodness –
Can barely stand,
So heavy with excesses.

Listen, to the way he moans –
How the next drawn breath
Whistles and wheezes
On the weight of weather.

See, how he staggers
With his load –
How his sack-full swagger
Bellies and buckles
With the heft of plenty.

He knows the score –
Has seen before
December's brittle ghost,
Hoary and heartless
With a fist of splinters.

Knows well the boast
Of swallows on the wing –
Wefting, like shuttles,
From the warp of winter.

When I think of November I think of Thomas Hood's poem of the same name: 'No warmth, no cheerfulness, no healthful ease, no comfortable feel in any member – no shade, no shine, no butterflies, no bees, no fruits, no flowers, no leaves, no birds - November!' - Or something along those dreary lines! This is the month when fog and frost start to return with a vengeance and if it's not foggy or frosty it's blowing a gale or pouring with rain – or both! The month starts off as it means to go on. The first day is All Saints – alleluia brothers! - and then the second day is All Souls – death and a sense of dreadful despondency. The Anglo Saxons called it *windmonath* for obvious reasons! Nevertheless, as dark and dismal as the month may be at times there is always something of interest to been seen and enjoyed by devotees of the fields and the river banks. The last leaves are falling in Ulting churchyard; the frost has nipped them and the wind is carrying them away. It's like a Danaëon shower – Zeus is casting gold upon the waters. The brunt sou'westers scour the river's surface and scudding clouds and rifts of sporadic blue are reflected in the weather's shattered mirror. Once more the robin sings – the only voice in the maelstrom; the epitome of hope, however sad its woe-begotten music. Robins of both sexes not only sing both by day and by night, but unusually they also defend their own territories throughout the winter months. Robins and roach, my two totem animals, my two defining principles of nature and the spirit, who remain integral parts of my holistic system of thought through all of the twelve inspirational months of the year. Robins and roach – God's Word manifested – epiphanies of redemptive light; alleluia brothers and sisters – alleluia! The weather's atrocious; the trees' gnarled and arthritic limbs rattle in the blast and the torrential rain spatters across the river in wind-driven silver swathes. I decide that the weather's perfect for a day in town – away from the wilds and wastes of a chill November countryside. I drive along the bleak and desolate back roads where greenness is all but a memory and rooks are hurled like discarded leather gloves into the relentless roistering of the wind and incessant rain, and make my way to the ancient town of Maldon.

One of the oldest towns in Essex the pre Saxon, Romano-British Maldon was built on flat land to the north of the Chelmer near to what is now Heybridge. Roman remains revealed little until works for a residential development carried out in 1994 exposed evidence of a large temple and an extensive market area that probably flourished between c 50 BC and AD 200. The settlement was abandoned in the 5th century due to rising water level and much of the area is now just rough grazing land. In AD 916 the Saxons established a burgh on high ground to the south of Heybridge, close to the lowest crossing points for both the rivers Blackwater and Chelmer. At the time it was a very important town with its own mint and a population of about 1000. In 991 one of the most famous battles in England took place: 'The Battle of Maldon' which is remembered in one of England's earliest surviving Anglo Saxon poems. Brythnoth, the Earl of Essex, defended the causeway to Norsey Island against the invading Danes. Brythnoth and his army were doing well until the Danes said that it wasn't fair to fight on the causeway and that they would prefer to fight in the open. Why Brythnoth agreed to their demands we'll never know but the unfortunate consequence was that he and many of his men were killed and England came under the yoke of Dane Geld. By the Middle Ages Maldon had become a large market town serving the surrounding area. Many trading vessels unloaded at a small quay at Fullbridge and others further downstream at The Hythe. One of the greatest periods of economic expansion was in the 18th century due to the increase of maritime trade. By 1800 expansion had taken place to such an extent that Maldon effectively became linked with the neighbouring village of Heybridge. The marshland between the two communities became an industrial complex and eventually in the 19th century the arrival of the railways opened up trade even more. Even when I was a boy you could travel from

Maldon by steam train directly to London or Southend-on-Sea by use of the so-called 'Wickford loop'. Unfortunately, Beeching and his axe put pay to both the glorious days of steam and cheap excursions to Southend and the City. The viaduct across the River Chelmer remained an impressive sight for many years but even that has gone the way of the steam trains. Many Medieval buildings survive including: the Moot Hall (the former Town Hall) and the Blue Boar in Silver Street has been a hostelry since at least 1632. Prior to that it was the home of the Essex family the De Veres and the inn sign is derived from their heraldic coat of arms. Lawrence Washington, the great, great, grandfather of George Washington, the first President of the United States of America, is buried in the ancient church of All Saints. Industry was extensive: boat and barge building flourished as did fishing and flour milling. In 1795 William Bentall (a local yeoman farmer) established a foundry in Heybridge to produce his soon to be nationally famous 'Goldhanger plough'. John Sadds, the timber and builder's merchants were also ship owners and wharfingers in the town at one time and are still part of my abiding memory of the place. In the latter part of the 19th century Cooks the boat builders was established. They were famous for the many small craft they built and also some larger vessels including the well known Thames barge 'Dawn'. They are still there down by The Hythe and specialise in repairing and rebuilding the majestic and stately Thames barges in their own dry dock. The heyday of the railways and the canals has come and gone and heavy, motorised transport has taken their place. Nevertheless the town has been by-passed by a new road and as a consequence of that fact many of the larger vehicles have no need to come into the town and it therefore still retains much of its original character – long may it so remain.

November the 5th and Guy Fawke's night is with us once again. The rain of All Saints and All Souls has finally eased and with luck the bonfires that have materialised all the way from

Chelmsford to Maldon and Heybridge Basin will be just about dry enough to allow the celebrations to commence. Being brought up as a Catholic I was forbidden to join in the fun and frolics of the number one pyrotechnic night of the year because of Guy Fawke's association with Catholicism, but of course I was more than prepared to risk the ignominy of mortal sin and the subsequent torments of excommunication and hell and eternal damnation to claim my place in the as good as pagan explosive and 'conflagratory' festivities! Over the years I have spent the occasional Bonfire Night beside the canal on my own. One I particularly remember was a clear, starlit night blessed with the sparkle of an exceptionally severe frost. I stood on the bridge at Paper Mills and waited for the fireworks to begin. A full moon was reflected in the river and the dreadful torpedoed shape of a large pike crossed the moon sinuously, with its muscular antithesis of lucky silver. What cold and unsuspecting fish will suffer the same inevitable fate as the luckless Guy Fawkes tonight – I thought? And then with a shiver I turned from the terminal abyss of the ripple-less and reflective waters and looked towards the brighter prospects of Danbury Ridge. Rockets started to rise into the clear and starlit heavens and began to expand into bursts of explosive colour. The glow of innumerable bonfires stipple the hillside with their ghastly emanations and a succession of loud retorts fractured the frosted silence. The distant stars competed with their own form of celestial pyrotechnics as they shimmered with iridescence and dowsed and tempered their fiery silver steel in the ice-encrusted depths of the Navigation. Disturbed coots and moorhens responded with raucous complaints and a quartering barn owl feathered the dense, debacle of the air with hushed, enlightened wings. It was cold – so cold. My breath was condensing heavily and as it rose into the frosty night it seem as though my own ghost was escaping into the endlessness of space. I could hear the occasional fish splash on the river's surface as it failed in its efforts at levitation. It was time to head for home and the welcoming hearth. Where the river had been in spate a few days earlier the meadows were covered in a sheet of glistening ice. The rosehips and hawthorn berries in the hedgerows were coated in spicules of frost and the leaves on the ground were furred and sparkling in the moonlight. Again a robin was singing – they're always singing – whatever the month, whatever the weather. I walked up North Hill past Poleighs and on towards the Rodney where I'd left my car. It was still early enough for a pint of best bitter before I finally made my way home. The pub was warm and welcoming, the pint, slightly chilled and delicious, and out through the frosted windows starlight and fireworks speckled the moonlit sky with the diffuse and multicoloured magic of a November night to remember and revere.

November's flower is the chrysanthemum, a bloom which I personally have always found to be very funereal. At this time of year the graveyard urns in All Saints at Ulting and St Mary the Virgin at Little Baddow are often full to overflowing with these sad yet unbelievably beautiful flowers. Death and dying are the very aspect of November. On the 11th we not only commemorate the dead of two World Wars and those still dying in conflicts across the globe, but coincidentally it is also Martinmas – the day of St Martin; the patron saint of soldiers. From Martinmas right through to St Andrew's day (the patron saint of Scotland) on the 30th of the month our unpredictable climate can produce some of the gloomiest weather imaginable. To walk through the riverside copses in the fog as the transparent silver droplets on the trees – heavy with their inverted worlds – fall at the slightest breath of air and spatter the fallen leaves with sounds reminiscent of some miniature tattoo, can be a damp and dismal experience never to be forgotten. The river could easily be the Styx and the boat that comes eerily out of the fog could have Charon at the helm – with Hades as its dreadful destination. Anglers are fishing for pike in the weir pool at Paper Mills – a fish as portentous of death as the rapacious sharks that roam the warmer waters of the world.

There are some monstrous pike in the River Chelmer and 'red in tooth and claw' seems their one and only *raison d'etre!* Pound for pound they're a fantastic fighting fish though and to get a take while spinning is the epitome of atavistic excitement. You could easily be a Palaeolithic hunter/gatherer as you stare into the primeval jaws of this most deadly of fishes. It's easy to imagine the last great Ice Age – the vast and varied landscape all around you was formed by that very climatic phenomenon. How would we cope with winters like those of long ago when the river was frozen solid for 6 months of the year, plants leafless and sparse, and the ground impervious to any amount of digging with flint, wooden, or antlered implements? Nowadays it's said that we're in the midst of a period of global warming and it has to be admitted that in the last decade or so frost and snow have been nowhere near as prolific as they used to be. Nevertheless, as they say, the only thing that's predictable about the British weather is its unpredictability and it's not unknown to see snow in November or the river frozen over even now. Not so many years ago I went to a funeral in late November and six inches of freshly fallen snow covered the mournful ground beside the grave: even this year (2004) we had one or two nights of severe frost towards the end of the month and the cuts at both Paper Mills and Hoe mill were crisped with the thin crystalline slithers of sun-deflective ice. Fog and frost, wind and rain, and the occasional short spell of sunlit and warming respite are this month's inveterate and inalienable legacy to the rambler and the fisherman alike – and like it or not, if you want to enjoy your sport or the countryside in November you have to put up with the vagaries and chill vicissitudes of the deities of water in all its many and varied forms. As I cast a spinner into the weir at Paper Mills and allow it to sink and draw as I retrieve it, I see its submerged silver shape and think of the star that will take its place when December reaches its dark and holy nadir. November has come to its cold inevitable end and we must prepare ourselves for the deeper cold to come. A small jack pike lunges at my lure and the rod bends accordingly. The fight is fast and furious as it 'walks on its tail' and the river's inviolable crystal is smashed like a sacred icon in the hands of Cromwell's rebellious army; but Advent is upon us and the yearly restoration of our latent spirituality and holiness is - for once at least - imminent and assured.

Hoe Mill lock

River or road? – Hoe Mill

Winter spate between Hoe Mill and Ricketts lock

153

Author with dogs in the snow - Ulting

After the 'hurricane' 1987 - Ulting

No fishing today – the author - Ulting

River Blackwater – Wickham Bishops

The navigation looking west from Heybridge

Looking east from Heybridge

DECEMBER
POEMS:

DECEMBER RAIN

The weather changes for the worse –
Turns wet and mild.

All thoughts of snow have thawed –
The mind, like ice, dissolving under rain.

The seasonal denial, tradition thwarted –
Not even frost or starlight to expose
That winter need for unaccustomed whiteness.

The arthritic trees complain –
Gesticulate in grey, prevailing torment.

The sullen clouds, like cynical balloons,
Deflate at dusk and saturate the senses.

DILUVIAL

The River's in flood again –
Has had enough
Of summer's slow meander.

It inundates the fields –
Pretends a sea
Where cattle sailed all year

And swished their tails
Through semaphores of sunlight.
December's clouds

Are wrung by sullen hands –
Are fists of scud
That beat the season's bounds

And drown the leaves, unhinged
By prone sou'westers.
The gulls drift far inland –

Flake down, like snow
Incongruous with sound,
To settle on the shrub-infested waters.

A rift of gold
Turns wavelets into scales –
A sudden fish, that leaps, and then submerges.

MIDNIGHT MASS

We're on the verge of Christmas:
Foxes bark
And the lights from trees
In warm domestic windows
Taint the snow:

The mist, the moon, stained glass
And carols in the freeze
Of vaulted stone
As candles catch the crystals in the glow
Of midnight bliss.

We're on the verge of Christmas:
A robin sings
A dirge all on his own
As snowflakes fall - like feathers -
Angel's wings - from lunar clouds:

The moon, the stars, the ring
Of changing weather
Where water turns its countenance to bone
And love is born from winter's frozen shroud
Without a kiss.

December comes in with the full legacy of a drear November, only this time the fog is freezing. This is winter in earnest. The trees stand like enormous frozen ghosts against the blue-suffusing sky above the river. Upwards is the only direction. At eye level everything is dimmed and diminished. Silence is the only sound – the world is voiceless. But it's beautiful – unbelievably beautiful: blue and grey and white, tinged with a hint of gold. I'm in Ulting churchyard again – this is my special place; my spiritual ground. A starling settles in the tallest ash tree and a fine descending shower of frozen particles dusts my hair and shoulders with its chill, unbidden weightlessness. It's nearly noon and still below freezing and the ice continues to thicken on the canal. Suddenly an unexpected skein of Canada geese drift in and out of vision as they drag their ghostly chains of sound towards the blear and frozen lakes beside Hoe Mill. Everything seems as though it's been made by an angelic host of hyperborean confectioners. A spiritual northern breath has decorated the whole of the limited landscape with a glint and reflective icing sugar. The holly and hawthorn blister with scarlet berries and the faint yet glimmering sunlight gilds the imaginary edges of this cold and grey-encompassed cake with its barely emphatic seasonal sparkle. The frost in the graveyard is as thick as snow and the molehills take on the appearance of a miniature Alpine range. If I saw a troll, right now, right here, I would neither be surprised nor alarmed – it would seem perfectly natural; in a supernatural sort of way! As the afternoon wears on the fog begins to thin a little and although low in the sky the less impeded sunlight glitters through the frosted landscape and quickens the hue of a deep cerulean sky. The remission will not last; the temperature must already be around minus 3° centigrade and is still falling fast. The fog will thicken up again for sure; the moon will become a blurred and eerie ghost, and the fox and the quartering owl bestow the far, the faint, and the only audible voices in the dense and gathering darkness.

December alternates between extremes. After the freezing fog comes the rain – the incessant and torrential rain. Three drenched and diluvial days have left the navigation bursting at the seams with the slick and viscous equivalent of liquid chocolate. At Hoe Mill what defences there were, were breached by early afternoon, and the river has spilled across the roadway and the water meadows. The three country routes across the river at Boreham, Little Baddow and Hoe Mill, will by now be impassable and local travellers will have to drive the long ways round if they wish to complete their journeys. I walk along the raised wooden footway beside the road and watch as the powerful swirling flood waters transfer from one lake to another. The valley between Hoe Mill and Beeleigh has in relatively no time at all become an inland sea. Fish roam where some of them have never roamed before while others with longer subaqueous memories forage again in the faint-remembered pastures of their past. Roach become sub aquatic herbivores as they graze through the sodden cattle meadows and pike like the lions in some watery savannah as they prowl across the predatory grasses. The rain is heavy and continuous and doesn't want to abate. It's the worst winter spate for many years and by rights I shouldn't be enjoying the spectacle – but I can't help myself. There is something about meteorological extremes that moves me deeply. Not that I'd wish to experience earthquakes or tornadoes and the likes, nor for that matter wish them upon anyone else, but there's something deeply satisfying about a flood, a blizzard, freezing fog, or a drought and a heat-wave! Why this should be I couldn't tell you for certain – excitement engendered by a change from the norm, the feeling of security watching the tremendous powers of nature from a safe vantage, or just sheer *joie d'vivre* – who knows? Eventually the rain stopped and the waters started to subside. It will take a few days or more before the river is back to its normal level and in the meantime the gulls will take advantage of the unexpected seascape and the fish continue to forage in their new-found watery pastures. When the water finally recedes the land will be covered with sand and silt and the soil be subsequently enriched. Stranded molluscs will litter the newly exposed landscape and the large swan mussels, as large and black as a leather purse, with their contents of flesh and occasional pearls will be a welcome winter supplement for passerine and waterfowl alike - and anything else that's hungry. The waters come and the waters go – it's all part of the inevitable cycle of the year; earthquakes and erupting volcanoes gave the earth the gases it needed for the sun to produce our atmosphere and floods are the unavoidable consequence of an unalterable system of natural affairs. The earth in all its guises takes life admittedly, but it also gives life and nourishes existence with its generous abundance. We have to die that others may live – it's inescapable. When you look at extremes in the climate and the vicissitudes of the earth, remember we're here because of them; they're not here because of us! Yes, there is suffering, and we must do all we can to limit its affects on humanity and the rest of nature's creation; but ultimately this is the dream, reality is elsewhere. In truth no matter what the pain or what the suffering it is only a temporary, temporal and material phenomenon, life is with the stars – always was and always will be. You were never born so in truth you can never die – this is a dream my friends, a short and fantastic dream. Enjoy what you can; transcend what you can't – after the flood the dove and the raven returned with their olive branches. The sun will shine again, the river sparkle in the low yet lyrical light, and God will bless the hunter and the hunted with a love that knows no bounds – like a living spate in our cold and wet Decembers.

I am standing in the lane by Beeleigh Abbey and looking out across the mudflats and the saltings of the tidal River Chelmer towards Maldon and the Blackwater Estuary beyond. December sees an influx of bird life along the coastal margins. Shelduck laugh hysterically; redshank tweke, oystercatchers bleep and curlew flute their lost and lonely calls. Here the navigation meets the sea and the avian exchange is wondrous to behold. Fieldfares and redwings feed on hips and haws and the ivy's blackened berries in amongst the trees and the hedgerows while whooper swans newly arrived from the tundra graze contentedly in the greening meadows. The occasional purple sandpiper pipes as its name demands, knot and dunlin and turnstones scurry at the edge of the tide, and bar-tailed godwits vie with the little egrets and the herons for the tastiest morsels the ever-abundant mudflats have to offer. Lapwings travel west in large sunlit and coruscating flocks and garrulous rooks caw continually from the surrounding tree tops. December is not a dead month – life is profligate and prolific. I speak to a lady who rents one of the cottages owned by the Foyle family of Beeleigh Abbey; she has only lived there for six months but has already fallen deeply in love with the place – and who wouldn't? The garden is lush with trees and shrubs and surrounded by marshes, reeds, mudflats, saltings and tidal and freshwater – a paradise indeed! I walk down the lane to the falls; it's barely 3 o-clock in the afternoon and the light is already beginning to fade. We are moving towards the winter solstice and the shortest day of the year. Solstice: *Sol the sun* and *stice* stands still. The sun stands still for three days before it starts to rise again – a rerun of Easter; Christ was crucified and rose again on the third day – a coincidence – maybe, maybe not. The Pagan and the Christian have a habit of reflecting each other and the season of Yule is no exception to that infallible rule. A robin sings; its breast has been pierced by a thorn and its melancholy song is a seasonal requiem. Water trickles over the falls and the weir and a strange, until now unnoticed star, buries its quickening silver in the water's contracting womb. It is time to go home, to bring in the evergreens, and to decorate the tree. The uncanny star seems to follow me as I walk back along the lane towards the car – more golden now than silver; more mysterious than purely astronomical. 'Time is away and somewhere else' as the brilliant Northern Irish poet Louis MacNeice once wrote. He also wrote about 'the drunkenness of things being various'. Did he like me have that unfathomable sense of unity in diversity – was he equally attracted by the particular and the general? This star is timeless and yet it is here in time – how can it be; how can love become incarnate? I make my way along the shadowy country lanes and the moon appears like a vast, primeval snowball in the dark and velvety void. Soon I will be at home, the fire will be lit and the decorations will be twinkling in the shadows. 'If winter comes can spring be far behind?' Will a God be born, or a man, or the ever-faithful once and eternal golden sun? As I enter the driveway the first frost is glistening on the grass and I can hear a blackbird scratching in amongst the dry leaves under the hedge as it searches for food. I open the front door, look up at the lingering star, and pray like I've never prayed before.

At Ulting the church is decorated for Christmas. The tall, resin scented fir tree is not only decorated with lights, baubles and a star, but is also festooned with various types of corn dolly – the old customs die hard. The Advent wreath stands in a place of honour. Four red candles – one for each Sunday in Advent – are entwined with holly and ivy; and in the middle one tall, solitary white candle waits to be lighted at midnight on Christmas Eve. The holly symbolises the male principle – the ivy the female. Joined they become one with each other and the 'Light of the World'. It's sunny and warm for the time of the year and outside on the river bank and angler is fishing with a roach pole. In general anglers are very friendly people so I walk across to talk to him. The roach lie deep at this time of the year and are much more difficult to catch than in the summer. I ask him how he's doing and he informs me that he's had a reasonable catch with some good quality fish amongst them. I watch him as he trots the middle track; his float dips imperceptibly, he strikes and he's into another good fish. The sunlight is glittering on the river's surface skin and a missel thrush sings from the top of a half-denuded oak. Soon it will be Christmas Eve and my thoughts turn to the eternal Gift bringer. Old Father Christmas wreathed in evergreens, Santa Claus dressed in a red robe and drawn through the frosted sky by reindeer, the Three Wise Men: Caspar, Melchior and Balthazar, are all well known nowadays but how many people know that the tradition of gift bringing is as old as Odin when he rode through the winter night on his eight legged horse Sleipnir to distribute bounty to his people? I always go to midnight mass on Christmas Eve, not at Ulting unfortunately; I live too far away, but at another church also called All Saints in Southend-on-Sea. Although I might be some ten miles away as the 'Gift Bringer' flies my mind is never far from the river bank. Once I purposely went to spend Christmas Eve by the navigation. It didn't snow but at least it was cold, clear, starlit and frosty – as near to traditional as can normally be expected in these latitudes. Midnight mass wasn't being held at Ulting church and it had probably been transferred to the mother church at Hatfield Peverel. I didn't mind, my religion was to be the starlight and the recumbent hook of a glimmering crescent moon. I still believe in Father Christmas – If you imagine something it's real as far as I'm concerned. I gazed longingly into the mystery of the starlit skies and awaited the confirmation of my ever-hopeful faith. A sleigh, an eight legged horse, or three exotic and strangely levitating Wise Men – it didn't matter, not in the slightest. A heron flew across the river and to me it was Odin's eight legged steed. An owl hooted and the sky was alive with Santa's avuncular laughter. A badger scuttled through the undergrowth and Old Father Christmas drifted across the churchyard loaded with the fruits of summer. Was it all real? What's real and what isn't in this temporal dream of ours? It was real to me and that was all that mattered! All the church bells in the vicinity rang out across the pale and frosted meadows and that lingering golden star I saw earlier in the month had finally come to earth – was Love incarnate. 'I saw three ships come sailing in on Christmas day in the morning'; was it at Collier's reach, were the Three Wise Men at the helm of a schooner bearing their gifts of gold and frankincense and myrrh - or was it just coal and timber and lime? Who knows – who will ever know this side of the veil of heavenly mysteries? I think I'm already in heaven. The horses are garlanded with evergreens along the towpath and the spectral barges are lit by flickering candlelight. Sounds of 'silent night' and *'adeste fideles'* drift along the misted surface of the river and people in Chelmsford and Maldon and Heybridge and all the towns and villages between – whether awake or sleeping – are touched by the redemptive power of 'peace and goodwill to all men'. The midnight river flows towards the Blackwater estuary and dawn and the son of all suns waits in the silent, shivering northern sea to surface and surprise us with his/its glory.

Christmas is over and the New Year beckons with snow and an easterly wind. The circle is complete. In the grounds of Ulting church snowdrops and crocuses are buried treasure waiting to be unearthed. At St Mary the Virgin in Little Baddow the amelanchier is budding and the Virgin's wild flower garden is gestating spring and summer in its dark and earthy womb. Sandford lock is frozen and Barnes Mill is deep in snow but the winter jasmine defies Boreas and his cold, uncharitable breath and kindles golden starlight out of ice. At Beeleigh the weir can't comb its frigid hair but water trickles somewhere in a brook and a song thrush tries to sing a warming song. I walk along the bank between Hoe Mill and Ricketts lock; the snow is deep and difficult to negotiate and enormous smoking snowdrifts spill from the hedgerows with their Arctic fancies. A lone swan is white on white as it traverses the frozen landscape and occasional voiceless blackbirds counter with contrast from the bleak and berried hedges. Brythnoth and the White Canons share a drinking horn in Maldon and Richard Coates drinks a glass or two with his navvies in the Black Boy at Chelmsford. I stand in the midst of a white and wasted wilderness as the snow falls horizontally and the river slips, like history, under ice. When did this story begin – when will it end – who knows? The journey was one of 'Reflections' and now as the river blears over with the weight of ice the reflections must end. 'Twelve Months – Twelve Moods', a lifetime of love for this riverine corner of England condensed between the pages of one small book. 'History and Imagination' on 'The Chelmer and Blackwater Navigation' taking the reader through the spiritual and material depths of time and timelessness as seen in the mirror of this glorious

English river. Turn from the pages of this book and make your own inimitable journey along the towpaths and the country byways of the Chelmer's incomparable valley and I'm sure that you, as I, will fall for its ever-persuasive rural charms and be hooked like the roach and the gold-encrusted chub. Business or pleasure – it doesn't matter. The river flows from the northern hills of Essex to the sea; and time and the realms timelessness wait in the darkening deeps that haunt the mind and the fish-enlightened shallows of a dream.

The author and Clare Harvey – the Hythe – Maldon